# THE EURO:
## A CURRENCY OF 300 MILLION PEOPLE

# THE EURO:
## A CURRENCY OF 300 MILLION PEOPLE

SERGE K. GUNYÉ
EDITOR

**Novinka Books**
*New York*

**Senior Editors:** Susan Boriotti and Donna Dennis
**Coordinating Editor:** Tatiana Shohov
**Office Manager:** Annette Hellinger
**Graphics:** Wanda Serrano and Matt Dallow
**Editorial Production:** Alexandra Columbus, Maya Columbus, Alexis Klestov,
Vladimir Klestov, Matthew Kozlowski and Lorna Loperfido
**Circulation:** Ave Maria Gonzalez, Vera Popovic, Luis Aviles, Sean Corkery,
Raymond Davis, Melissa Diaz, Meagan Flaherty, Magdalena Nuñez,
Marlene Nuñez, Jeannie Pappas and Frankie Punger
**Communications and Acquisitions:** Serge P. Shohov
**Marketing:** Cathy DeGregory

*Library of Congress Cataloging-in-Publication Data*
*Available Upon Request*

ISBN: 1-59033-908-8.

Copyright © 2004 by Novinka Books, An Imprint of
Nova Science Publishers, Inc.
400 Oser Ave, Suite 1600
Hauppauge, New York 11788-3619
Tele. 631-231-7269    Fax 631-231-8175
e-mail: Novascience@earthlink.net
Web Site: http://www.novapublishers.com

All rights reserved. No part of this book may be reproduced, stored in a retrieval system or transmitted in any form or by any means: electronic, electrostatic, magnetic, tape, mechanical photocopying, recording or otherwise without permission from the publishers.

The publisher has taken reasonable care in the preparation of this book, but makes no expressed or implied warranty of any kind and assumes no responsibility for any errors or omissions. No liability is assumed for incidental or consequential damages in connection with or arising out of information contained in this book. Any parts of this book based on government reports are so indicated and copyright is claimed for those parts to the extent applicable to compilations of such works.

This publication is designed to provide accurate and authoritative information with regard to the subject matter covered herein. It is sold with the clear understanding that the publisher is not engaged in rendering legal or any other professional services. If legal or any other expert assistance is required, the services of a competent person should be sought. FROM A DECLARATION OF PARTICIPANTS JOINTLY ADOPTED BY A COMMITTEE OF THE AMERICAN BAR ASSOCIATION AND A COMMITTEE OF PUBLISHERS.

*Printed in the United States of America*

# CONTENTS

| | | |
|---|---|---|
| **Foreword** | | vii |
| **Chapter 1** | Background on the Euro<br>*Tatiana Shohov* | 1 |
| **Chapter 2** | The Euro<br>*Ian F. Fergusson* | 19 |
| **Chapter 3** | The Euro Currency: How Much Could it Cost the United States?<br>*Gail E. Makinen* | 25 |
| **Chapter 4** | The Euro: Implications for the United States - Answers to Key Questions<br>*Thomas J. McCool and Susan S. Westin* | 33 |
| **Chapter 5** | The Impact of the Changeover to the Euro on Community Policies, Institutions and Legislation<br>*European Commission:*<br>*Economic and Financial Affairs* | 87 |
| **Chapter 6** | Meeting in the Composition of Heads of State or Government<br>*Council of the European Union* | 97 |
| **Index** | | 109 |

# Foreword

On January 1, 2001, the Euro became the official, circulating currency of twelve of the fifteen nations of the European Union, replacing such national currencies as the franc, the mark, and the lira. It becomes the currency of just over 300 million people encompassing an economic area with a GDP of $5.2 trillion. The common currency is a pivotal step in the economic integration of participating European Union member states. A successful European common currency may also provide a challenge to the dollar as the world's reserve currency.

The Federal Reserve estimates that upwards of $350 billion in U.S. currency now circulates outside the United States. If this is redeemed for the Euro, the United States will have to buy back its currency and, in the process, provide goods and services up to this amount to foreigners. In addition to this one-time cost, the United States will forego the annual seigniorage it now gets from these dollar holdings, estimated at between $15 billion and $20 billion per year.

The book presents issues and analyses related to this new and powerful currency.

*Chapter 1*

# BACKGROUND ON THE EURO

## Tatiana Shohov

## THE EURO CLOSE UP: CONVERSION TO THE EURO[†]

On January 1, 2002, the euro banknotes and coins were introduced in 12 Member States of the European Union, with seven different banknotes and eight coins. The countries adopting the Euro are Austria, Belgium, Finland, France, Germany, Greece, Ireland, Italy, Luxembourg, The Netherlands, Portugal, and Spain. Denmark, Sweden, and the United Kingdom will not be changing from their local currencies to the Euro at this time.

Each EU member nation making the change to the Euro will phase in the new Euro currency separately. The EU Central Bank's Internet web site has complete information in several languages, including English, about each country's conversion schedule (http://www.euro.ecb.int).

The Euro will become legal tender in all twelve countries. Local currencies will still be accepted as legal tender for most financial transactions for a period of time. However, in the twelve listed countries, automatic teller machines (ATM's) will begin to issue Euros, banks will provide Euros for foreign currency exchange and vendors have been encouraged to provide change in Euros as of January 1. Delays in financial transactions may result during the initial stages of the transition.

---

[†] Excerpted from http://www.euro.ecb.int/en/section.html and http://travel.state.gov/euro.html websites.

Effective January 1, U.S. Embassies and Consulates located in the twelve "Euro" countries will accept only dollars and the new currency, Euros, for fee-based services.

The arrival of the euro, however, means much more than exchanging one currency for another. It involves individuals and businesses not only in the countries that have joined the single currency, but all over the world.

It is in all our best interests to familiarize ourselves with the look and feel of the euro banknotes and coins.

The new coins – 50 billion of them – have one side common to all 12 countries and a reverse side specific to each country, while the 14.5 billion banknotes look the same throughout the euro area. Altogether, the banknotes and coins produced total over €664 billion.

So, whether you are in Europe or elsewhere in the world, why not take a journey with us to discover how the euro evolved?

## HISTORY OF THE EURO

The new currency has been years in the making.

The Treaty of Rome (1957) declared a common European market as a European objective with the aim of increasing economic prosperity and contributing to "an ever closer union among the peoples of Europe".

The Single European Act (1986) and the Treaty on European Union (1992) have built on this, introducing Economic and Monetary Union (EMU) and laying the foundations for our single currency.

The third stage of EMU began on 1 January 1999, when the exchange rates of the participating currencies were irrevocably set. Euro area Member States began implementing a common monetary policy, the euro was introduced as a legal currency and the 11 currencies of the participating Member States became subdivisions of the euro. Greece joined on 1 January 2001 and so 12 Member States introduced the new euro banknotes and coins at the beginning of this year.

The successful development of the euro is central to the realization of a Europe in which people, services, capital and goods can move freely.

This is history in the making. It is the largest monetary changeover the world has ever seen – join us in celebrating and finding out more about our new currency.

# How did the Euro Evolve

Our new single currency originates in the Treaties. All the Treaties were prepared and signed by members of the European Council, which comprises the Heads of State or Government of each of the Member States of the European Union (EU), and then ratified by each country according to national legislative procedures.

The elected governments of Member States together created and developed the euro. In Madrid in December 1995, the European Council adopted the name "euro".

The European Central Bank (ECB) was established on June 1, 1998. It is based in Frankfurt am Main, Germany, and aims to maintain price stability and to conduct a single monetary policy across the euro area.

This is done through its own activities and through working with the national central banks. Together, the ECB and the euro area national central banks are known as the Eurosystem.

# The European System of Central Banks

The national central banks (NCBs) of the European Union, along with the European Central Bank (ECB), make up the European System of Central Banks (ESCB).

The NCBs of Member States not participating in the euro area, i.e. Denmark, Sweden and the United Kingdom, have a special status which allows them to conduct their own national monetary policies, but not to take part in deciding and implementing monetary policy for the euro area.

## *The Eurosystem*

The national central banks of the euro area together with the ECB are known as the Eurosystem.

The Eurosystem's primary objective is the maintenance of price stability. It meets its objectives through:

- deciding and implementing monetary policy;
- conducting foreign exchange operations;
- and operating payment systems.

The NCBs of the participating Member States played a key role in the smooth transition to the euro. Their responsibilities have included:

- introducing the euro in their respective countries;
- managing the changeover from national currencies to the euro;
- creating the necessary systems to effectively circulate the euro banknotes and coins;
- withdrawing national currencies; and
- providing advice about and promoting the use of the euro.

## EURO BANKNOTES

On January 1, 2002, seven banknotes were introduced in 12 Member States of the European Union.

- there are seven new banknotes
- they have the same design throughout Europe
- each banknote has a different colour and different size
- the EUR 5 is the smallest banknote and the EUR 500 the biggest.
- The banknotes circulate in denominations of EUR 5, 10, 20, 50, 100, 200 and 500.

On the front of the banknotes, windows and gateways symbolize the European spirit of openness and co-operation. They have pictures of windows, arches, gateways and bridges on them as well as a map of Europe and the European flag. The 12 stars of the European Union represent the dynamism and harmony between European nations. They were designed by the Austrian artist Robert Kalina.

To complement these designs, the reverse of each banknote features a bridge. The bridges symbolize the close co-operation and communication between Europe and the rest of the world.

These designs, and the following features, are presented in more detail below:

- the name of the currency – euro – in both the Latin (EURO) and the Greek (EYPO) alphabets;
- the initials of the European Central Bank in five linguistic variants – BCE, ECB, EZB, EKT and EKP – covering the 11 official languages of the European Community;
- the symbol © indicating copyright protection; and
- the flag of the European Union.

14.89 billion euro banknotes have been produced; 10 billion were needed to replace the national banknotes in circulation and nearly 5 billion are to be held in reserve.

**20 Euro Front**

**20 Euro Rear**

**50 Euro Front**

**50 Euro Rear**

**100 Euro Front**

**100 Euro Rear**

## Euro Coins

The eight denominations of coins vary in size, color and thickness according to their values, which are 1, 2, 5, 10, 20 and 50 cent or EUR 1 and EUR 2. One euro is divided into 100 cent.

Luc Luycx of the Royal Belgian Mint won a European wide competition to design the euro coins. One side of each coin features one of three designs common to all 12 euro area countries showing different maps of Europe surrounded by the 12 stars of the European Union.

The reverse side of each coin shows individual designs relating to the respective Member State, surrounded by 12 stars (see Country-specific faces, or click on the relevant country's flag). Euro coins can be used anywhere in the euro area, regardless of their national sides.

Milled edges have been introduced to make it easier - especially for those with impaired sight - to recognize different values. Sophisticated bi-metal technology has been incorporated into the EUR 1 and EUR 2 coins which, together with lettering around the edge of the EUR 2 coin, prevents counterfeiting.

## Common Side/Country-Specific Side

The front of each coin has the same design for all 12 countries in the euro area. The reverse side displays different designs for each country, created by their own national artists. All coins can be used anywhere in the euro area.

## From Design to Distribution

Years of planning and preparation are behind our new banknotes and coins. From the design of the euro symbol to the logistics of distributing billions and billions of euro across 12 participating Member States: find out here how the euro symbol was born, how the banknotes and coins were designed, how the production of the new money has been organized and how it was introduced and distributed.

## Euro Symbol Design

The euro symbol was created by the European Commission as part of its communications work for the single currency. The design had to satisfy three simple criteria:

- to be a highly recognizable symbol of Europe
- to be easy to write by hand
- to have an aesthetically pleasing design.

Thirty or so drafts were drawn up internally. Of these, ten were subject to a qualitative assessment by the general public.

Two designs emerged from the survey well ahead of the rest. It was from these two that the then President of the Commission, Jacques Santer, and the European Commissioner in charge of the euro, Yves-Thibault de Silguy, made their final choice.

## Here is How the Euro Symbol was Born

It was inspired by the Greek letter epsilon, harking back to Classical times and the cradle of European civilization. The symbol also refers to the first letter of the word "Europe". The two parallel lines indicate the stability of the euro.

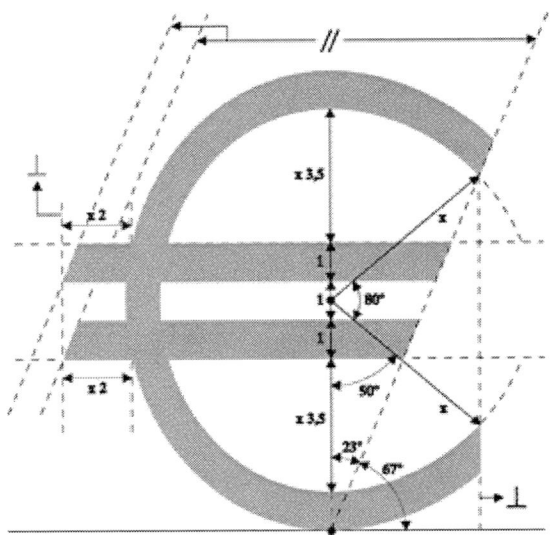

The official abbreviation for the euro is EUR and this has been registered with the International Organization for Standardization (ISO).

## Banknote and Coin Design

### Design of the Euro Banknotes

In February 1996, the Council of the European Monetary Institute (EMI), the forerunner of the ECB, launched a competition to design the euro banknotes. National central banks nominated designers to sketch a series of seven banknotes, using one or both of two nominated themes: "Ages and styles of Europe" and an abstract modern theme.

Later that year, a panel of renowned experts in marketing, design and art history drew up a shortlist of the five best designs in the two categories. A public opinion survey on the shortlisted designs was conducted across Europe.

The winning designs were by Robert Kalina of the Oesterreichische National Bank, inspired by the theme "Ages and styles of Europe", and were selected in December 1996 at the Dublin European Council. His theme depicts designs from seven important architectural periods in Europe's cultural history.

### Design of the Euro Coins

There are eight euro coins. Each euro coin has one side that is common to all 12 Member States. This design shows variations of the map of Europe. The designs for the European side were selected following a competition organized by the European Commission and were approved by the Ministers of the Member States.

The European side of the coins was designed by Luc Luycx of the Royal Belgian Mint and depicts a map of the European Union against a background of parallel lines linking the 12 stars of the European Union flag.

The 1, 2 and 5 cent coins show Europe's place in the world and the 10, 20 and 50 cent coins depict Europe as a group of individual nations. A united Europe without frontiers is represented on the EUR 1 and EUR 2 coins.

# Production

The Eurosystem is responsible for the overall production and distribution of the new banknotes. This means there is a partnership between the ECB and the national central banks.

## *Banknotes*

Production of the euro banknotes began in July 1999 in a number of euro area countries and today production is under way at 12 printing works across Europe - two in Germany and one in each of the other countries of the euro area, with the exception of Luxembourg.

14.5 billion banknotes are being produced with 10 billion going into circulation in January 2002 and 4.5 billion being held in reserve to accommodate any changes in demand for the banknotes.

## *Coins*

50 billion coins are being minted across the euro area. Production began in May 1998. Much work has been done to ensure that the new coins will meet vending machine standards across the euro area.

### How far advanced is the production of the euro banknotes?

Production of the new banknotes is now well under way. The production will be completed in time for the changeover on 1 January 2002. Each national central bank decided where to print its initial run of banknotes. Precise common standards and strict quality controls have been applied, as it is imperative that the euro banknotes display the same visual appearance.

### Why is it necessary to have a reserve of 4.5 billion euro banknotes?

Reserve stocks are part of good planning. At any point in time, the national central banks must be able to satisfy the demand for banknotes. A careful watch is being kept on the levels of electronic and credit spending, as this affects the amount of paper currency in circulation. Demand for banknotes fluctuates and the national central banks need to be prepared to handle this effectively.

### Who bears the cost of printing the euro banknotes?

The national central banks are responsible for bearing the cost of the initial supply of euro banknotes.

# What is the breakdown of the 14.5 billion euro banknotes being produced between the 12 countries?

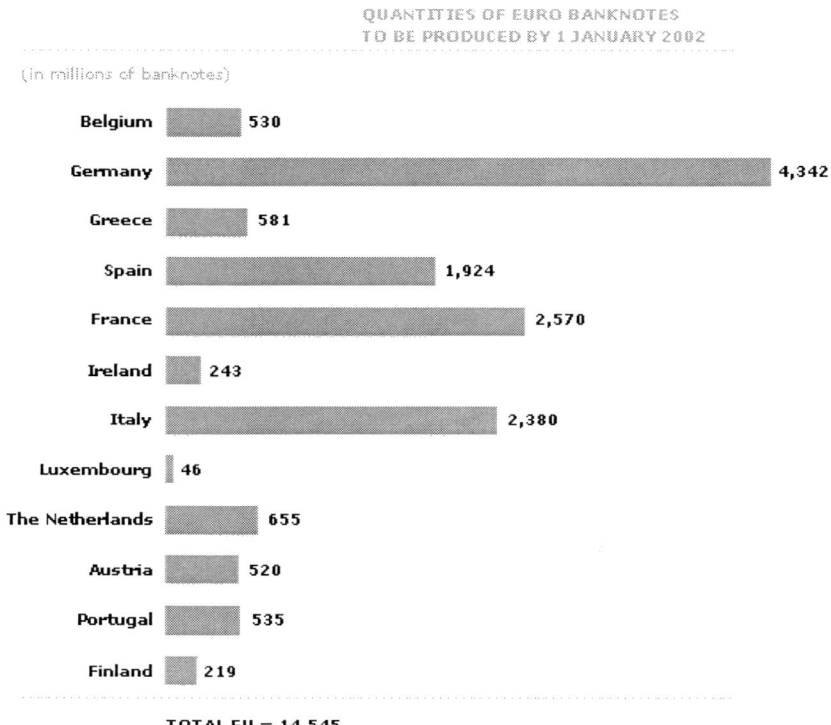

QUANTITIES OF EURO BANKNOTES
TO BE PRODUCED BY 1 JANUARY 2002

(in millions of banknotes)

|  |  |
|---|---|
| Belgium | 530 |
| Germany | 4,342 |
| Greece | 581 |
| Spain | 1,924 |
| France | 2,570 |
| Ireland | 243 |
| Italy | 2,380 |
| Luxembourg | 46 |
| The Netherlands | 655 |
| Austria | 520 |
| Portugal | 535 |
| Finland | 219 |

TOTAL EU = 14,545

## What is the breakdown of euro banknotes by denomination?

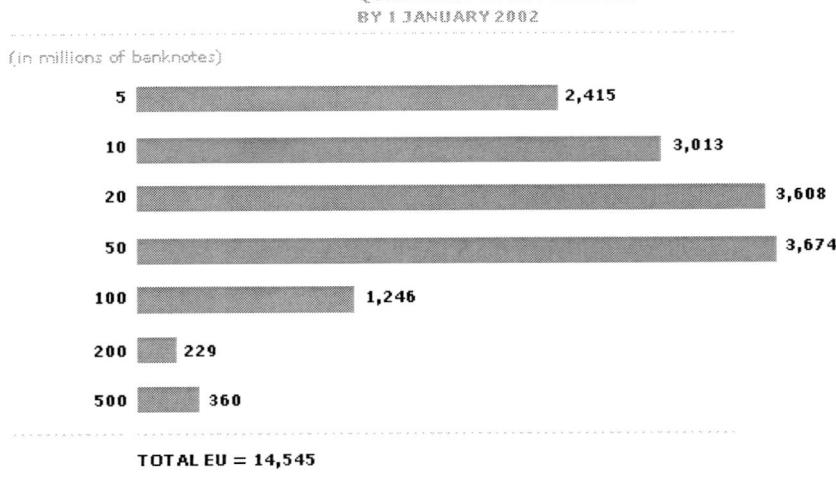

## Who decides how many coins to produce?

The European Central Bank is responsible for approving the overall value of coins to be issued. The use of coins varies greatly across the euro area, so each Member State has estimated the number of coins it needs and justified that figure to the European Central Bank, which has authorized the appropriate level of production.

## What is the breakdown of the 50 billion euro coins being produced between the 12 countries?

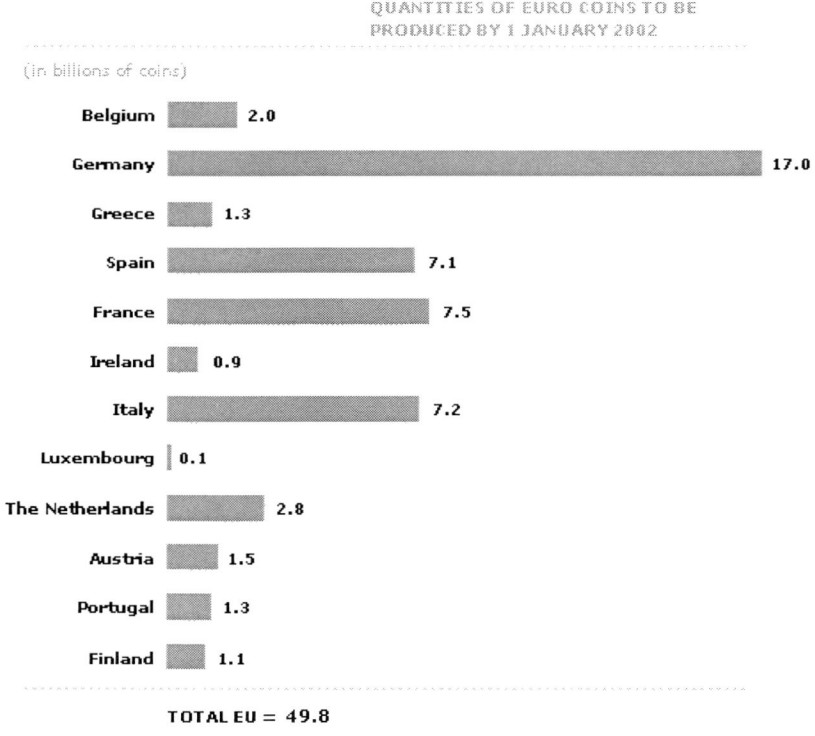

QUANTITIES OF EURO COINS TO BE PRODUCED BY 1 JANUARY 2002

(in billions of coins)

|  | |
|---|---|
| Belgium | 2.0 |
| Germany | 17.0 |
| Greece | 1.3 |
| Spain | 7.1 |
| France | 7.5 |
| Ireland | 0.9 |
| Italy | 7.2 |
| Luxembourg | 0.1 |
| The Netherlands | 2.8 |
| Austria | 1.5 |
| Portugal | 1.3 |
| Finland | 1.1 |

TOTAL EU = 49.8

## What is the breakdown of euro coins by denomination?

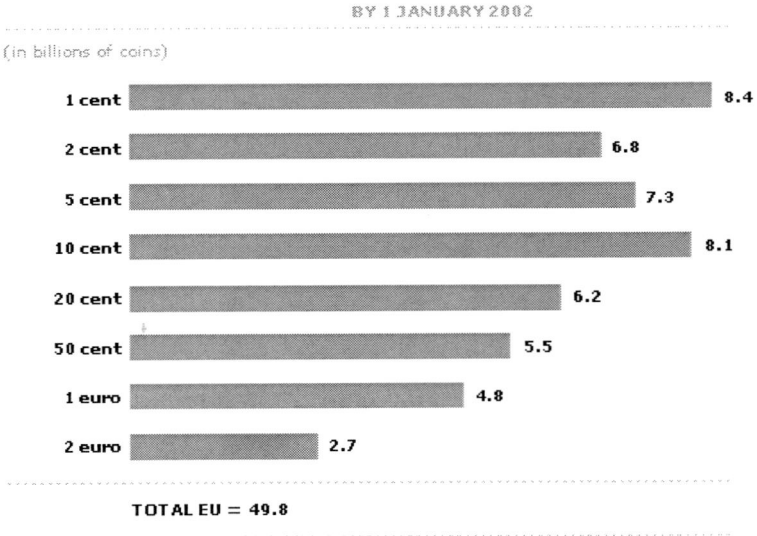

## Distribution of Banknotes and Coins

All currency issued by participating national central banks after 1 January 2002 will be new euro banknotes and coins.

### *Will the speed of changeover be the same in all countries?*

In most participating countries, the "dual circulation period" will last between four weeks and two months. After that, national banknotes and coins will cease to be legal tender, and the euro banknotes and coins will become the sole currency throughout the euro area.

Once the "dual circulation period" is over, you will still be able to exchange your national banknotes and coins for euro banknotes and coins at your national central bank either indefinitely or for a very long period of time (at least ten years in the case of banknotes). Concerning national coins, in most cases this period is limited to a few years.

### *Who is responsible for distribution of the new money?*

The European Central Bank (ECB) is responsible for managing and overseeing the successful changeover of currencies while the national central banks (NCBs) are responsible for drawing up national changeover plans according to each Member State's capacities and cash-distribution systems.

## Will any euro cash be available before 1 January 2002?

To facilitate the changeover, cash-handling organizations such as banks, post offices, cash-in-transit companies, vending machine companies and retailers across the euro area will receive euro cash toward the end of 2001. The extent to which this will take place, the timing and the quantities involved will vary between Member States.

The second half of December 2001 will see limited quantities of euro coins made available to the public in some parts of the euro area. It will be possible to buy euro coins in the form of starter kits at banks, post offices and, in some countries, at retail outlets. The starter kit will be an assortment of all the euro coins in a small bag. The starter kits will help consumers to familiarize themselves with the new coins. They will also enable a significant part of the public to make purchases using the exact change in euro as from 1 January 2002. This will help avoid cash bottlenecks in the retail trade and shorten waiting times at checkouts.

## Will all Automated Teller Machines (ATMs) issue euro banknotes as from 1 January 2002?

ATMs, along with banks, are the principal means of distributing banknotes to the public across Europe. As such, they will play a key role in the speedy changeover to the new euro banknotes.

In many countries, the banks have committed themselves to adapt the software and hardware of ATMs in such a way that some machines will already dispense euro banknotes as of Monday 31 December 2001, at midnight. In these countries, the rest of the machines will be adjusted to dispense euro banknotes during Tuesday, 1 January 2002. This will ensure a rapid supply of euro banknotes to the public.

This means that banks and Automated Teller Machines (ATMs) will begin to put euro banknotes into circulation on 1 January 2002. You will receive your change in euro when shopping with your national currency during the changeover period.

Banknotes and coins will be distributed to key institutions such as banks and post offices towards the end of 2001 in preparation for the changeover. Ministries of the Interior and police forces are drawing up special security measures across the euro area to address any security risks associated with such large-scale distribution of cash.

## RECOGNIZING THE EURO

### Banknotes

Various security features have been incorporated into the euro banknotes. They will help you to recognize a genuine banknote at a glance.

### Feel

Feel the "raised" print – the special printing processes give banknotes their unique feel;.

### Look

Look at the banknote and hold it up to the light: the watermark, the security thread and the see-through register will then be visible. All three features can be seen from the front and the reverse side of genuine banknotes.

### Tilt

Tilt the banknote: on the reverse side, if you tilt the banknote, you can see the brilliance of the iridescent stripe (on the low-value banknotes) or the color-shifting ink (on the high-value banknotes).

On the front of the banknote, you can see the shifting image on the hologram foil stripe (on the low-value banknotes) or the hologram foil patch (on the high-value banknotes).

## CONVERSION RATES

The conversion rate for the euro for each participating currency is irrevocably fixed and is the only rate to be used for conversion either way between the euro and the national currency unit or for conversion between the national currency units.

The euro conversion rates are:

| Belgian franc | 40.3399 | Deutsche Mark | 1.95583 |
| Greek drachma | 340.750 | Spanish peseta | 166.386 |
| French franc | 6.55957 | Irish pound | 0.787564 |
| Italian lira | 1936.27 | Luxembourg franc | 40.3399 |
| Dutch guilder | 2.20371 | Austrian schilling | 13.7603 |
| Portuguese escudo | 200.482 | Finnish markka | 5.94573 |

## Euro Area

The euro area encompasses those Member States of the European Union in which the euro has been adopted as the single currency and in which a single monetary policy is conducted under the responsibility of the decision-making bodies of the European Central Bank. The euro area currently comprises Belgium, Germany, Greece, Spain, France, Ireland, Italy, Luxembourg, the Netherlands, Austria, Portugal and Finland.

## Euro symbol (€)

The graphic symbol for the euro was inspired by the Greek letter epsilon and refers to the first letter of the word "Europe". The parallel lines represent the stability of the euro. The official abbreviation for the euro is EUR, which has been registered with the International Organization for Standardization (ISO) and is used for business, financial and commercial purposes.

## European Central Bank (ECB)

The European Central Bank was established on 1 June 1998 and is situated in Frankfurt am Main, Germany. It ensures that the tasks conferred upon the Eurosystem and the European System of Central Banks (ESCB) are implemented either by its own activities pursuant to the Statute of the ESCB or through the national central banks.

## Eurosystem

The Eurosystem comprises the European Central Bank (ECB) and the national central banks of the Member States which have adopted the euro in Stage Three of Economic and Monetary Union (EMU). There are currently 12 national central banks in the Eurosystem. The Eurosystem is governed by the Governing Council and the Executive Board of the ECB and has assumed the task of conducting the single monetary policy for the euro area since 1 January 1999. Its primary objective is to maintain price stability.

## European System of Central Banks (ESCB)

The European System of Central Banks (ESCB) comprises the ECB and the national central banks of all 15 Member States of the European Union. It includes, in addition to the members of the Eurosystem, the national central banks of the Member States which have not adopted the euro. The ESCB is governed by the Governing Council, the Executive Board and the General Council of the ECB.

## Economic and Monetary Union (EMU)

The Treaty establishing the European Community sets out the process of achieving Economic and Monetary Union in the European Union in three stages.

Stage One of EMU started in July 1990 and ended on 31 December 1993. It was mainly characterized by the dismantling of all internal barriers to the free movement of capital within the European Union.

Stage Two began on January 1, 1994. It provided for, inter alia, the establishment of the European Monetary Institute (the forerunner of the European Central Bank), the prohibition of financing of the public sector by the central banks and of privileged access to financial institutions for the public sector, and the avoidance of excessive deficits.

Stage Three started on January 1, 1999 with the transfer of monetary competence to the Eurosystem and the introduction

*Chapter 2*

# THE EURO

## Ian F. Fergusson

### ISSUE

On January 1, 2002, the Euro became the official, circulating currency of 12 of the 15 nations of the European Union, replacing such national currencies as the franc, the mark, and the lira. On March 1, the transition period to the new currency officially ended, and the legacy currencies can no longer be used for transactions. The Euro is now the currency of just over 300 million people encompassing an economic area with a GDP of $5.2 trillion. The common currency is a pivotal step in the economic integration of participating European Union member states. A successful European common currency may also provide a challenge to the dollar as the world's reserve currency.

The Euro's introduction proceeded relatively smoothly. Conversion of the Eurozone's ATMs were completed within the first week. Reports from several countries indicate that despite some check-out delays and shortages of small denomination currencies, European consumers adopted the currency more readily than expected. Traumatic scenarios of currency shortages, robberies, and consumer panic never materialized, and it was estimated that most transactions were being conducted in Euros by the second week of introduction.

## BACKGROUND

The introduction of the Euro may prove to be a pivotal moment in uniting the economies of the 12 countries of the European Union that have adopted it (Denmark, Sweden, and the United Kingdom remain outside of the Eurozone, see below). However, the ground has been long prepared for this moment. The Treaty of the European Union (the Maastricht Treaty, signed in 1992) created the European Monetary Union (EMU) and its successor, the European Central Bank (ECB), that now determines monetary policy for the 12 countries of the Eurozone. The treaty detailed the economic convergence requirements that countries needed to achieve to be eligible to participate in monetary union. These criteria included a stable currency and exchange rate, an inflation rate and interest rates within a strict band relative to other EMU countries, government budget deficits within 3% of gross domestic product (GDP), and government debt at no more than 60% of GDP. In March 1998, 11 countries had achieved these criteria and became members of the EMU. (Greece subsequently "converged" and met the requirements in March 2001.)

The adoption of the Euro has several economic policy implications for national member governments. On January 1, 1999, the Euro was introduced as a currency of account, its value determined as a weighted value of participating national currencies. National governments no longer set monetary policy within the Eurozone. National central banks such as the Deutsches Bundesbank or the Banque de France continue to exist as units of the ECB, but monetary policy is set uniformly by the ECB. European national governments had differing authority to influence (or direct) the monetary policy of their central banks; now they have none. Monetary policy is determined by two reference points: growth of the money supply and the rise in consumer prices. The goal of the ECB is price stability in the short and medium term. Therefore, members states cannot use monetary policy to affect short-term economic conditions. Maastricht criteria on budget deficits and debt/GDP ratios also limit national governments from affecting economic performance through fiscal policy. These restrictions may cause tensions among member states with different levels or concepts of government services and different economic conditions.

Three nations of the European Union have not joined. Denmark rejected the Euro in a referendum on September 28, 2000. However, the value of Danish kroner is tied to the Euro through a managed float arrangement. Sweden and the United Kingdom have also held back. The recent election in Sweden returned the pro-Euro Prime Minister Goran Persson to office, and the government is planning to hold a referendum on joining the currency in 2003. The British government has also watched the development of Euro from afar. The Conservative government of Prime Minister John Major signed the Maastricht Treaty that established the blueprint for monetary union in 1991. However, the government insisted on a clause establishing the right to withdraw from the EMU, which it subsequently exercised during a currency crisis in 1993. The present Labor government of Prime Minister Tony Blair has declared that it will propose a referendum on adoption of the Euro at a time when five economic conditions are favorable to U.K. accession. During the election, the Conservative party campaigned forcefully against the Euro and further European integration. Although the Conservatives were roundly defeated, public opinion in Britain has continued to oppose adopting the Euro. Demand for Euros in each of the three countries is reported to be strong, however, with many retailers accepting the Euro.

## Economic Challenges

The introduction of the Euro as the sole circulating currency of 12 of the member states of the European Union has been called the largest peacetime logistical operation in history. Aside from the physical challenge of minting new coins, printing new bills, and distributing this currency to thousands of banks, ATMs and retail outlets, the changeover may present several other economic challenges as well.

Inflation. Some economists fear that the Euro's introduction may set off about of inflation in the Eurozone resulting from the translation of millions of prices into Euros. Each outgoing currency has a fixed exchange rate with the Euro, yet each price may not correspond to a Euro denomination. Hence, that price must be rounded up or down for the price to be expressed in Euros. Prices must be converted not only at the retail level, but intermediate and input prices must be changed as well. The cumulative effect of rounding prices upward would be inflation: both to Eurozone economies and those that trade with them. However, any inflation resulting from this exercise would be a one time, non-recurrent phenomenon. Anecdotal evidence indicates that this upward rounding did occur, yet it did not have a significant impact on aggregate consumer prices.

The Single Market. The Euro can be seen as a visible symbol of the single market, the creation of which is an enduring commitment of the European Community. The single market has also been manifested by the abolition of frontier controls, free movement of people and goods, harmonization of national regulations, and the establishment of European jurisprudence. However, in some areas markets remain remarkably national. For example, wide price differentials exist among member countries for many like products. Aside from local tax differences and different transportation costs, producers have been free to charge what each national market will bear because it has been too difficult or too time consuming for consumers to make price comparisons between currencies. The Euro will introduce transparency to the pricing structure, and considerably rationalization of prices between countries is expected.

International Considerations. On its introduction on January 1, 1999, the Euro traded at $1.18. By November 2000, the abstract currency had fallen 31% to $.82. However, the currency broke through the 1 euro - 1 dollar mark briefly during the summer of 2002, and has recently traded around $.98. It has also fluctuated against the British pound and other major currencies. Several reasons have been put forward to explain this volatility. Before the economic slowdowns on both sides of the Atlantic, the dollar's strength was attributed to foreign capital inflows, and higher growth and greater productivity resulting from greater structural flexibility in the U.S. economy. During the current recession, investors have responded positively to the U.S. Federal Reserve's effort to rekindle economic growth through cuts in interest rates. In contrast, the European Central Bank has tended to follow the former German Bundesbank's emphasis on controlling inflation rather than promoting growth through monetary policy. In addition, some have criticized the ECB for unclear policy signals and excessive secretiveness. Since the September 11, 2001 terrorist attacks, the dollar initially lost approximately 3% against the Euro, but then recovered to pre-attack levels as investors engaged in a "flight to quality" by purchasing U.S. assets. See Terrorism Briefing Book, International Capital Flows, by James K. Jackson. There has also been speculation that the Euro's weakness is a consequence of the market's initial overvaluation of the currency.

The population of the Eurozone and the size of its economy most likely will make the Euro a major currency. Some observers and policymakers have expressed the possibility that a strong Euro could displace the dollar as the world's primary reserve currency. The country possessing the reserve currency has the advantage of a greater degree of fiscal and monetary policy autonomy, and also of its use in commodity pricing and international transactions. As a reserve currency, the dollar also benefits from seignorage, a condition occurring when a nation's currency is widely held overseas. Currency overseas that is not redeemed for U.S. goods and services acts as interest-free debt, thus saving the U.S. Treasury from issuing bonds or paying interest for the amount of foreign holdings. If the Euro supplants the U.S. dollar as a currency of value, the U.S. Treasury loses the seignorage, the U.S. economy would have to redeem dollars with goods and services, and reduced demand would lower the value of the dollar.

*Chapter 3*

# THE EURO CURRENCY: HOW MUCH COULD IT COST THE UNITED STATES?

## *Gail E. Makinen*

On January 1, 1999, the European Monetary Union introduced a new currency called the Euro. Initially, it is a unit of account or a common denominator for expressing the prices of the goods and services of the member countries. Later, Euro currency notes will be introduced and it will become a circulating currency. It is at this point that it could become costly for the United States. This will occur it the Euro currency proves to be a good substitute for the dollar currency now in circulation outside the United States. Federal Reserve estimates suggest that upwards of $350 billion in U.S. currency now circulates outside the United States. If this is redeemed for the Euro, the United States will have to buy back its currency and, in the process, provide goods and services up to this amount for foreigners. In addition to this one-time cost, the United States will forego the annual seigniorage it now gets from these dollar holdings, estimated at between $15 billion and $20 billion per year.

## THE EURO

On January 1,1999, the European Monetary Union introduced its new currency the Euro. Initially it will function as a unit of account or a common denominator for expressing all of the goods and services sold by the member countries of the Union. Later, in 2002, Euro denominated currency and coins will be introduced.[1] It is the introduction of the Euro as a circulating currency that has important and potentially costly implications for the United States. Should the Euro currency prove to be a good substitute for the U. S. dollar notes held abroad, the United States would be forced to redeem those dollars and this redemption would involve both a large one-time cost and a smaller continuing cost to the American taxpayer. Additionally, the meaning attached to the monetary aggregates as indicators of U.S. monetary policy might become more uncertain complicating the oversight responsibility the Congress has with respect to monetary policy.

## How Much American Currency is Held Abroad?

The answer to this question is mat we don't know with certainty. As the Fed reminds. us, "currency movements are difficult to measure for some of the reasons that currency is popular: It can be easily concealed and readily carried across borders, even in large quantities (a briefcase can hold $1 million in $100s)."[2] It is estimated that the sum is considerable. On October 8, 1998, the Federal Reserve stated: "We believe that as much as two-thirds of all Federal Reserve notes in circulation — perhaps $250 to $300 billion dollars — are now held abroad."[3] If the same proportion is still held abroad, it would now be close to $350 billion. A cursory examination of recent trends in the behavior of the currency component of the U.S. money stock, particularly since the early 1980s, suggests that the Federal Reserve's estimate may be on mark.

Measured in 1999 prices, per capita holdings of currency have risen from about $897 dollars in 1960 to nearly $1900 in 1999. This growth has been especially rapid in the last twenty years. For example, between 1960 and 1981, real per capita holdings rose from about $897 to $949, or about 6%. Between 1981 and 1999, they doubled or rose about 100%. Yet, over this nearly 40-year period, 1960-1999, the growth of branch banking,

---

[1] See also U.S. Library of Congress. Congressional Research Service. *European Monetary Union: an Overview*. CRS Report 98-535E, by Arlene Wilson.
[2] Porter, Richard and Judson, Ruth. The Location of U.S. Currency: How Much Is Abroad? *Federal Reserve Bulletin.* October 1996: p. 883.
[3] Estimate given by Theodore E. Allison, Assistant to the Board of Governors of the Federal Reserve System in testimony before the Subcommittee on Domestic and International Monetary Policy. October 8, 1998. This estimate appears to be an update of the work cited in footnote 1 above.

automated teller machines, and the use of credit cards, should have allowed people to economize on their use of currency, especially over the second half of this period, the period of the most rapid growth in real per capita currency holdings.

If we focus only on 1999, as noted above, per capita currency holdings average about $1900. This means that the typical American household consisting of, on average, 2.6 persons, would be holding nearly $5000 in currency Multiplied by the approximately 100 million households in circulation in 1999 suggests an aggregate currency holding by households of $500 billion. This is clearly very large and closely approximates the amount of currency in existence late in 1999. Yet, the Flow of Funds Accounts prepared by the Federal Reserve show that households and nonprofit organizations held, on average, during 1999, about $425 billion in the form of checkable deposits and currency. Since a large fraction of this sum is undoubtedly checkable deposits, it suggest that much of the currency in circulation is not held by American households.

Finally, if currency is used for the "small change" type transactions in our economy, it is surprising to find that 65% of the value of U.S. currency in circulation is in $100 bills (the sum is 75% if $50 bills are included). In Canada the sums are quite different. A little less than 5% of the Canadian money in circulation is in $100 bills while nearly 30% is in $50 bills; the total being 34.5% of the total value in circulation.[4]

These developments suggest that a large portion of U.S. currency is held outside of the United States. Having foreigners hold U.S. currency is a means by which America as a nation is able to use more goods and services than it produces. When and if the Euro is substituted for the dollar, that substitution will be the means for some reduction in the standard of living of Americans as America will then produce more goods and services than it uses.

## HOW DOES THE UNITED STATES GAIN WHEN ITS CURRENCY IS HELD BY FOREIGNERS?

The United States gains in two ways when its currency is held abroad. First, when foreigners acquire US. currency they must give up goods and

---

[4] The U.S. data are from the Treasury Bulletin, October 1998. The Canadian data are furnished by the Currency Education Unit of the Bank of Canada and reflect the notes in circulation on October 31, 1998. Since the price level in Canada is considerably above that in the United States, the real value of the Canadian $50 bill is closer to the U.S. $20 bill.

services in return. This can be done both directly and indirectly. The direct way is simply to exchange dollars for the goods and services. This is one way foreign dealers in illicit drugs, for example, acquire dollars. The indirect way works through the foreign exchange market, the exchange value of the dollar, and the U.S. balance of payments and is exactly analogous to the purchase of the interest-bearing debt of the Treasury. For example, assume that an Eastern European wishes to acquire dollar notes. His/her bank may acquire them in the foreign exchange market. This increases the net demand for dollars, leads to dollar appreciation which increases the cost of U.S. goods and services in foreign markets and reduces the price of foreign goods and services in the United States. As a result, foreigners spend less on U.S. goods and services (the value of U.S. exports falls) and American spend more on foreign goods and services (the value of U.S. imports rises). The resulting trade deficit (or smaller surplus) increases the amount of goods and services available in the United States. This is a **one-time** effect. Each dollar transferred abroad has a **one-time** effect on the foreign exchange value of the dollar and the amount of goods and services available to Americans.

The second effect continues **indefinitely.** When foreigners acquire U.S. currency, they are, in effect, making an interest free loan to the U.S. Treasury. They could have held interest-bearing U.S. debt, but chose, instead, to acquire non-interest bearing U.S. debt. Thus, the United States does not have to pay interest on the currency held abroad (as well as on currency held by both foreigners and Americans in the United States). If the amount held abroad is from $300 to $350 billion, and interest rates are between 5% and 6%, the U.S. Treasury and the U.S. taxpayer avoids debt servicing costs of some $15 billion to $20 billion per year. And this accrues on an **annual** basis as long as the money is held abroad. The technical name given this saving is **seigniorage** or the profit government earns from issuing money. For this calculation to hold, however, the currency sent abroad must be a **net addition** to the money supply, an addition in response to an increase in the world demand for dollars. If this is not the case, and the currency sent abroad merely conies out of domestic holdings, the seigniorage calculation above is inappropriate for total seigniorage is not increased by having foreigners hold dollars.[5]

---

[5] The total amount of currency in circulation will increase in response to an increase in the world demand for dollars if the monetary policy of the government seeks to avoid deflation or a fall in the price level. Interestingly, seigniorage earned on certain dollar holdings abroad might be thought of as a tax on drug dealers who prefer to conduct their business in currency. By increasing the world demand for currency, the U.S. government derives revenue that it would not otherwise receive. This increased revenue can be thought

## THE COST OF THE EURO TO THE UNITED STATES

The cost to the United States of the Euro depends on the degree to which the Euro notes become substitutes for the dollars now held abroad. If they are good substitutes, then the foreign demand for dollars will fall, the dollars will be returned to the United States, and the reverse of the above transactions will occur. The United States will then return, either directly or indirectly, the goods and services it acquired when the dollars went abroad. In this sense, the United States can be said to have broken even.[6] (This disregards the timing issue. On a present value basis, the claim can be made that the United States gained).

Once the dollars are returned and retired from circulation, the United States can no longer derive seigniorage from them. This does not require that the seigniorage earned in the interim be returned, however. That is a permanent gain for the United States; a gain that came from an interest free loan over the interval that the dollars were held abroad. The extent to which seigniorage is lost depends on the fate of the returned currency. If the Federal Reserve wishes to avoid the jump in domestic prices that will occur when the dollars are returned following the fall in the world demand for them, it must remove them from circulation. To do this, the Federal Reserve will have to sell an equal amount of government interest-bearing debt that it now holds. This will reduce the annual profits of the Federal Reserve and the seigniorage which is returned to the Treasury. To make up for this loss in revenue, the government will either have to impose additional taxes on its citizens, increase borrowing, or reduce expenditures. Either way, the loss in seigniorage will impose an additional burden on Americans.

It is not inconceivable that the cost of the Euro to the U.S. taxpayer on both a one-time and continuing basis could be in the billions of dollars.

## CAN THE UNITED STATES FORESTALL THE LOSS OF SEIGNIORAGE?

The $15 billion to $20 billion in seigniorage that is now estimated to be earned annually for U.S. currency held abroad is a revenue source that is

---

of as accruing from a tax on the wealth of drug dealers held in the form of American currency.

[6] Whether this is good or bad depends on what goods were initially acquired relative to what was given up. If the goods acquired were illegal drugs, it might be difficult to argue that the U.S. gained having its currency held abroad for some period.

worth protecting (the same can be said for the one-time gain noted above the accrues when foreigners add to their holding of U.S. notes). There are a number of things that can be done to enhance the quality of the dollar as an international store of value. The first is the maintenance of political stability. The more stable our political system relative to that in Europe, the more likely foreigners are to want to hold their wealth in dollars. The second factor is the economic stability of the United States in terms of price level stability and stability in the exchange value of the dollar for foreign currencies. To the extent that the monetary and fiscal policies are aimed at producing a stable price level or low rate of inflation, the more likely foreigners will be to want to hold an asset on which they earn no interest. Moreover, since foreigners may ultimately wish to exchange their dollars for other currencies, they will be worried about the real dollar exchange rate. The dollar's quality as an international store of value should be enhanced if its real exchange value is more stable than that of potential rivals. Avoiding destabilizing shifts in fiscal and monetary policy should contribute to this end.

The dollars use as a store of value may also be enhanced by its portability. To that end, the government may wish to consider issuing higher denomination bills. Currently, the $100 bill is the largest circulating denomination. It may be useful to offer a $500 denomination note.

## What Other Problems Does the Euro Create?

The Congress has oversight responsibility for monetary policy. As such, measures indicating the posture of monetary policy can serve a useful purpose in the discharge of that responsibility. Among possible measures are collections of assets called money. A desirable attribute of any monetary aggregate or measure of money is that it has a stable relationship to money spending. It this is present, it is possible to predict the growth in money spending from the growth in the monetary aggregate.

When the dollar circulates abroad, and variations in the amount that circulate abroad are not predictable, it can complicate the oversight responsibilities of Congress. A steady growth in a given monetary aggregate may have quite different implications for the growth in domestic spending depending on variations in the foreign demand for the dollar. Unfortunately, the four monetary aggregates used in the United States (the monetary base, Ml, M2, and M3) have as a component the currency and coin in circulation outside the banking system.[7] The foreign demand for the dollar can be expected to decline with the introduction of the Euro as a circulating currency. It seems unlikely that such variations will be predictable. Nevertheless, the introduction of the Euro and its successful substitution for the dollar could increase the amount of money spending forthcoming from any monetary aggregate and increase the uncertainty attached to its behavior This concern, however, may be "much ado about nothing." The Federal Reserve has managed to guide the U.S. economy through two long expansions even with monetary aggregates whose growth was not dependably related to the growth in spending.[8]

## CONCLUSIONS

The amount of U.S. currency in circulation suggests that some, perhaps most, of it does not circulate in the United States. When a nation's currency circulates abroad, it can gain on a one-time basis through a net addition to the goods and services it is able to use. It also receives an interest free loan from the foreign holders of its currency. This allows the nation to earn additional seigniorage on a continuing basis as long as the currency held abroad is a net addition to the nation's money stock.

When substitutes for the dollar arise, it is possible that the foreign demand for U.S. currency will fall. The new currency of the European Monetary Union, the Euro, is a good candidate for a substitute. As such, the United States may be called upon to redeem some of the estimated $300 to $350 billion in dollars now held abroad. This will necessitate a one-time cost to buy the dollars back and a continuing cost in terms of the seigniorage that will be lost when the dollars return and are withdrawn from circulation. There is no evidence at this time to suggest what fraction of the dollar notes held abroad would be exchanged for Euro notes when they come into existence. Thus, the possible loss of seigniorage, estimated above at up to $20 billion annually, must be regarded as an upper bound or worst case.

---

[7] The Monetary Base is the most currency intensive of the four aggregates. About 90% of this aggregate is currency. For Ml, M2, and M3, the percentage consisting of currency at the end of 1999 was, respectively, 46%, 11%, and 8%. Ironically, for the current economic expansion, the monetary base seems to have the best track record explaining the behavior of aggregate spending in the sense that its' growth rate can explain both how the expansion got underway and why it continues. The three M's can either explain how the expansion got underway or why it continues, but not both.

[8] For a discussion about the instability in the U.S. monetary aggregates, see *Monetary Aggregates: Their Use in the Conduct of Monetary Policy*. CRS Report 95-1139 by Gail Makinen. November 22, 1995.

When a nation's currency circulates beyond its own borders, it can complicate the use of monetary aggregates as indicators of the expected course to be taken by domestic spending. Such problems may have occurred in the United States. They do not appear to have been serious as the Federal Reserve has managed to guide the U.S. economy along two very long expansions during the 1980s and 1990s that were punctuated by a short and shallow recession.

*Chapter 4*

# THE EURO: IMPLICATIONS FOR THE UNITED STATES - ANSWERS TO KEY QUESTIONS

## *Thomas J. McCool and Susan S. Westin*

### PREFACE

On January 1, 1999, 11 of the 15 countries in the European Union (EU) adopted the euro as a common currency.[1] On the same date, the new European Central Bank (ECB) took control of monetary policy in these 11 countries. This strengthening of economic integration in Europe is generally viewed as a way to foster greater political integration in addition to achieving economic benefits for member countries. Monetary union has created in Europe a new, large economic entity that could become a powerful force in world economic and financial markets. Its emergence has raised questions about how the United States will be affected, in areas ranging from the dollar's role as an international currency to the effects on U.S. trade and the relative attractiveness of the United States to foreign investors.

---

[1] The 15 members of the EU are Austria, Belgium, Denmark, Finland, France, Germany, Greece, Ireland, Italy, Luxembourg, the Netherlands, Portugal, Spain, Sweden, and the United Kingdom (U.K.). Denmark, Greece, Sweden, and the U.K. have not adopted the euro.

For example, over the past half century, the U.S. dollar has been the primary world currency for business transactions, holdings of currency reserves at central banks, and private portfolios. Concerns have been expressed about whether the euro will change the dollar's role in these areas and, if so, what the implications will be for the U.S. economy. With regard to policymaking, the advent of the euro has implications for U.S. monetary policy because, although such policy is determined primarily by domestic economic conditions, the Federal Reserve does take international conditions into account when setting monetary policy.

Some experts have said that the largest effect of the creation of the euro will be the transformation of financial services in Europe. For example, they predict that European stock and bond markets will become more integrated over time and could rival those in the United States.

Because Europe is an important trading and investment partner of the United States, there has been considerable interest in whether the introduction of the euro could affect trading and investment patterns. A key determinant of any potential effects is the euro's influence on economic growth in Europe. Although the euro can potentially benefit growth, it also brings policy challenges to national governments and the EU, and conclusions on its growth effects may remain tentative for some time.

The advent of the euro has implications for how international economic policies are set and implemented, such as bringing about some changes in representation at G-7 meetings on economic policy.[2] Whether this deeper European economic integration could affect the balance of power in economic policy deliberations, such as trade negotiations with the United States, has been of interest to U.S. policymakers.

We undertook this review of the implications of the euro for the United States at the request of the Chairman of the Subcommittee on Domestic and International Monetary Policy of the House Banking Committee. Specifically, our objectives were to answer the following questions: (1) What is the euro and why is Europe moving to it now? (2) What are the potential effects of the euro on the dollar? (3) What are the potential monetary policy and exchange rate effects of the euro? (4) What are the implications of the euro for financial markets and institutions and their regulation? (5) What are the euro's implications for U.S. trade and investment with Europe? And (6) What are the implications of the euro for international economic policymaking?

---

[2] The G-7 consists of seven major industrialized countries that consult on general economic and financial matters. The seven countries are Canada, France, Germany, Italy, Japan, the United Kingdom, and the United States.

## WHAT IS THE EURO?

**Q. What is the single European currency and how did countries qualify for membership in the euro area?**

**A.** The euro is the new currency being used by 11 of the 15 countries that are members of the European Union (EU). (See fig. 1.1.) The euro area comprises these 11 countries. The euro area countries have a population slightly larger than the population of the United States and economies with a combined gross domestic product (GDP) about 75 percent the size of the GDP of the United States.[3] (See table 1.1.)

**Figure 1.1:** Members of the European Monetary Union and the European Union

**Source:** European Commission documents.

---

[3] GDP refers to the total value of goods and services produced in an economy in one year.

**Table 1.1:** 1999 Population and GDP of the Euro Area and the United States

|  | Population | GDP |
|---|---|---|
| United States | 272 million | $9.1 trillion |
| Euro area | 291 million | $6.7 trillion |

Sources: European Union, Central Intelligence Agency, Census Bureau, and Bureau for Economic Analysis

When the euro was launched on January 1, 1999, the 11 countries in the euro area locked their exchange rates to the euro, redenominated their national debt into euros, surrendered control of monetary policy to the European Central Bank (ECB), and began using the euro in electronic transactions.

Citizens of countries that have adopted the euro still use their national currencies, such as the German mark or French franc, in daily transactions. However, the values of these currencies are legally tied to the euro and do not fluctuate in relation to one another. Thus, the euro represents units of national currencies. For example, ×1 equals approximately 1.96 German marks (see table 1.2 for a complete list of currency values). This legal linking to the euro allows financial transactions between countries and new issues of national debt to be denominated in euros. Euro coins and currency are to replace the national coins and currency by June 2002 at the latest, at which time the old currencies are no longer to be used. According to the EU, most countries are planning to have national coins and currency replaced by the end of February 2002.

**Table 1.2:** Euro and National Currency Conversion Rates

| €1 equals approximately… | Value[a] | National currency |
|---|---|---|
| | 40.34 | Belgian francs |
| | 1.96 | German marks |
| | 166.39 | Spanish pesetas |
| | 6.56 | French francs |
| | 0.79 | Irish pounds |
| | 1,936.27 | Italian lira |
| | 40.34 | Luxembourg francs |
| | 2.20 | Dutch guilders |
| | 13.76 | Austrian schillings |
| | 200.48 | Portuguese escudos |
| | 5.94 | Finnish marks |

[a] All values rounded to two decimal places. Exact euro values require the use of six figures.
**Source:** European Council Regulation 2866/98, December 31, 1998.

The EU set out a number of requirements to qualify for membership in the euro area. Countries had to be members of the EU and comply with four general economic criteria: price stability, a sustainable government financial position, exchange rate stability, and convergence of long-term interest rates. Table 1.3 spells out these criteria in more detail.

**Table 1.3:** Euro Membership Requirements

| General criteria | Specific requirements |
|---|---|
| Price stability | Annual rate of consumer price inflation must be within 1.5 percent of average annual consumer price inflation from the three countries with the lowest inflation rate as measured by the Harmonized Index of Consumer Prices (HICP). |
| Sustainable government finances | General government deficit must be no more than 3 percent of GDP and show progress towards lowering general government debt to 60 percent of GDP. |
| Exchange rate stability | National currency participates in the Exchange Rate Mechanism (ERM) and observes the normal margins of the exchange rate mechanism without severe tensions or devaluations for 2 years. |
| Long-term interest rate convergence | Long-term interest rates must be within 2 percent of the average rates from the three countries with the lowest inflation rates as measured by the HICP. |

**Source:** Treaty on European Union.

The various institutions of the EU, including the European Commission, the Council of the European Union, the ECB, and the European Parliament, have different roles in determining which countries qualify for membership.[4] On the basis of their respective determinations and recommendations, on May 3, 1998, the Council of the EU confirmed that 11 countries would adopt the euro beginning in 1999.[5]

**Q. What is the relationship between the euro and European Economic and Monetary Union (EMU)?**

**A.** The euro is the most significant and far-reaching part of the larger initiative known as EMU. EMU is the effort by EU countries to more closely link their economic policies to achieve greater political and economic integration. EMU continues the EU's efforts to achieve a fully integrated single market in goods, services, labor, and capital within the EU. The requirements for EMU are spelled out in the Treaty establishing the European Community, as amended in 1992 and 1997 (hereafter referred to as the Treaty), and further refined in decisions made by the Council of the EU.[6] In general, EMU requires countries within the EU to implement economic policies that ensure stable prices, sound public finances and monetary conditions, and a sustainable balance of payments.

The euro is the most significant aspect of the monetary union. The membership requirements for the euro area and the provisions related to the ECB are subsets of the EU's treaty provisions and legislation pertaining to EMU. For example, the requirements for membership in the euro area described above are spelled out in the portion of the Treaty related to economic and monetary policy; protocols to the Treaty; and subsequent Council decisions, regulations, and resolutions.

EMU also has a number of provisions that are not directly related to the euro. For example, EU member states must coordinate their national economic policies and provide information to the EU on their national economies. Representatives from EU member states also meet periodically to discuss approaches to economic issues and other matters of common concern. For example, in recent years, EU leaders have met to coordinate national policies on job creation, taxes, and European security and defense

---

[4] The European Commission proposes policies and legislation, is responsible for administration, and ensures that provisions of the treaties and the decisions of the EU institutions are properly implemented. The Council of the EU is composed of ministers or heads of state and government representing the member states. The European Parliament comprises 626 members, directly elected in EU-wide elections for 5-year terms.

[5] The European Monetary Institute, the ECB's precursor, participated in the 1998 decisions. The ECB will participate in future decisionmaking on euro area membership.

[6] Decisions made by the Council of the EU are legally binding on all EU member states. Most decisions are made by majority vote, but some require unanimity.

policy. Those EU countries that have not adopted the euro still have to abide by most of the other requirements of EMU.

Despite EMU and the euro, governments still retain a high degree of regulatory and legislative control over large sections of their economies, including their labor markets, tax codes, and welfare legislation. National governments are also responsible for implementing fiscal policy.

However, countries' ability to use fiscal policy is restrained by EMU. The Stability and Growth Pact, adopted by the EU in 1997, clarified how the surveillance of national fiscal policies will be carried out in the EMU environment. The Pact requires countries to have budgets close to balance or in surplus in order to avoid breaching the 3 percent of GDP deficit ceiling, except during extreme recessions.[7] For countries that have adopted the euro, failure to do so could result in sanctions from the EU, ranging from public criticism to fines of up to 0.5 percent of annual GDP. In addition, all countries are required to submit annual plans to the EU showing how they will reach this goal.

**Q. What is the rationale for the euro?**

A. Government leaders from euro area countries cite a variety of political and economic reasons for adopting the euro. In general, these countries believe the euro supports the broader political goals of greater European economic and political integration. Some leaders also hope that the creation of a more robust European Union will enhance Europe's global position in the world relative to the United States.

From an economic perspective, the introduction of the euro eliminates potentially costly fluctuations among values of national currencies within the euro area. It also fosters integration of goods, services, and financial markets. Europeans also hope the stringent economic requirements to join the euro area and sustain EMU will provide discipline to national budgets and encourage structural change in their economies. In particular, some experts believe these requirements, which impose economic restrictions on national monetary and fiscal policy, could pressure countries to liberalize labor markets and make other structural changes in their economies that would allow labor and capital to move more easily among firms, industries, and member countries.[8]

---

[7] This provision was added to ensure that countries could increase spending during mild economic recessions and still not exceed the 3 percent of GDP deficit limit set by the Treaty.

[8] Some examples of potential structural changes include reforming labor laws to make it easier to hire, train, and fire workers; allowing greater labor mobility across the EU; and reforming pensions to reduce fiscal burden and allow portability across countries.

Individual countries have additional and varying national reasons for joining the euro. For example, German political leaders stressed that adopting the euro would demonstrate Germany's commitment to remaining closely tied to the rest of Europe.[9] French politicians noted that the euro and EMU could bolster Europe's global influence and ensure that France had a direct voice in European monetary policy.[10] Italian leaders stressed the increased economic credibility their country would gain by joining the euro area.

Greece did not meet the criteria for membership in the euro area in 1998 but, according to the EU, it may do so in spring 2000 when its performance will be assessed again. The U.K., Denmark, and Sweden chose not to adopt the euro.

### Q. Why are four EU countries not in the euro area?

**A.** Although the U.K. meets the fiscal, inflation, and interest rate criteria for the euro, it has not tried to join the euro area, in part, because political leaders and the public have not been willing to give up the British pound and control over monetary policy. In 1991, the British negotiated a provision in the Treaty exempting the U.K. from the euro.[11] Support for the euro in the U.K. remains low, with one January 2000 poll showing that those opposed to joining the euro area outnumber those in favor of joining by about two to one. The U.K. does not plan to join the euro area until it has achieved greater economic synchronization with the rest of the EU.[12] The government has also pledged that any decision to adopt the euro must be ratified by the public in a national referendum before going into effect.

In 1992, voters in Denmark rejected the proposed amendments to the Treaty that had been negotiated in Maastricht. This created a political crisis within the EU because all EU member states had to approve the proposed amendments before they could go into effect. Thus, Denmark could have

---

[9] The political negotiations over the euro took place in the later 1980s and early 1990s, at precisely the same time Germany was reunifying. Other countries in Europe were concerned that a larger Germany could dominate the continent.

[10] Before the euro, the German Bundesbank (Germany's central bank) was viewed as, de facto, setting monetary policy for the rest of Europe. Because the German economy was so much larger and the mark was viewed as the strongest currency, other EU countries who had entered the ERM felt pressure to follow the lead set by the German central bank.

[11] Modifications to the Treaty on Europe must be approved by all member countries. The U.K. would not approve the changes necessary to implement the euro unless it was allowed to opt out.

[12] The U.K. government says that monetary union membership is contingent on five tests: (1) compatibility of the U.K. business cycle with the rest of Europe, (2) ability to react to problems with sufficient flexibility, (3) impact on foreign direct investment in the U.K., (4) impact on national financial services, and (5) implications for growth and employment.

entirely stopped EMU. To avoid this, the EU exempted Denmark from having to join the euro area. Danish voters approved the amended treaty in 1993. Currently, according to public opinion polls, the majority of the Danish public supports adopting the euro, and the government plans to hold a national referendum on eventual membership.

Sweden joined the EU in January 1995. Two years later the Swedish government decided Sweden should not join the euro area because of lack of popular support. However, unlike Denmark and the U.K., Sweden does not have a special opt out clause in the Treaty. To avoid membership in the euro area, the Swedish government ensured it would not meet the exchange rate criteria for membership. The ruling party has since come out in favor of joining the euro area, but it has not yet set a date for a national referendum on the issue.

Greece wanted to join the euro area but could not meet the economic requirements. The Greek government, backed by a solid majority of the population who support joining the euro area, plans to reapply in March 2000 in an attempt to gain membership in 2001.

**Q. Is the euro sustainable?**
**A.** Most experts maintain that there are many reasons to believe the euro is sustainable. Adopting the euro has been a top political priority of the euro area governments. Although ruling political parties have changed during this time, political support for the euro has not, even though some countries had to implement sometimes painful economic policies to join the euro area. Many experts told us that the current political leaders in the euro area countries and the EU will not allow the euro to fail.

However, some analysts have observed that the euro's sustainability will not be known until it has been tested by stress or even an economic crisis, especially a crisis that affects member countries differently. If the public believes that their country is suffering additional economic harm from the euro, there could be greater pressure on political leaders to back away from their support for the euro. Some experts have also pointed to the euro's potential for creating greater political and economic strains among national governments. For example, national leaders will no longer be able to use monetary policy or reductions in exchange rates to soften the impact of economic shocks. In addition, the EMU requirement to maintain a roughly balanced budget places some limits on the ability of national governments to spend more money to provide fiscal stimulus during economic downturns.

As a practical matter, it would be very difficult for a country to withdraw from the euro area. Many experts believe that the economic disruptions of leaving the euro area and recreating a national currency could outweigh the possible benefits of regaining a national currency and national monetary policy. Politically, there are no provisions in the Treaty for a country to voluntarily withdraw, nor are there processes for removing a country against its will. If a country left the euro area, it would violate the Treaty and likely trigger a political crisis within the EU.

According to experts, failure to maintain the euro area would have far-reaching consequences for Europe and the rest of the world. Most agree that only a major economic or political crisis could bring down the euro area. The collapse of the common currency would create economic uncertainty in Europe with likely spillover effects onto the rest of the global economy. Politically, failure of the euro area would be a major setback for the EU. According to many analysts, it would bring EU enlargement to a halt and undermine the credibility of other EU initiatives.

**Table 1.4:** Chronology of Selected Events Surrounding the Euro

| Date | Event |
|---|---|
| March 1957 | Six European countries sign the Treaty of Rome, establishing the European Economic Community (EEC). |
| January 1962 | Council adopts first regulations establishing common market in agriculture. |
| July 1968 | Customs union completed, common external tariff established, and freedom of movement guaranteed for workers within the EEC. |
| February 1986 | The 12 members of the European Community sign the Single European Act. The act extends the powers of the Community and establishes framework for a single market. |
| June 1989 | European Council calls for negotiations on treaty revisions necessary for the introduction of EMU and the euro based on plan developed by governors of central banks and Commission President Delors. |
| February 1992 | Maastricht Treaty signed by EU heads of state and government. |
| 1992-1993 | Treaty ratified by EU member states. |
| 1993-1997 | Countries reduce inflation and cut budget deficits to meet euro membership criteria. |
| 1994 | European Monetary Institute created as the precursor to the ECB. |
| June 1997 | EU adopts the Stability and Growth Pact. |
| May 1998 | Council of the EU announces participating countries. |
| January 1, 1999 | ECB begins operations as a central bank. Irrevocable fixing of conversion rates to euro. National debt converted into euros. |
| By January 1, 2002 | The euro notes and coins are to be introduced among the participating countries. |
| By June 2002 | National currencies are to be withdrawn, and only euro notes are to be legal tender. |

**Source:** European Union.

## How Could the Euro Affect the Dollar As An International Currency?

**Q. What is an International Currency?**

A. An international currency is one that is used for payments and finance outside the issuing country's borders. In the case of the U.S. dollar, for example, a sizeable amount of international trade that never crosses our borders is invoiced and paid for in dollars. Banks outside the United States take deposits and make loans in dollars. Dollar-denominated bonds are issued outside the United States. U.S. dollar currency notes circulate in substantial amounts in some foreign countries, sometimes for illicit purposes. In addition to these uses, which largely involve private sector entities, foreign central banks hold dollars as part of their official reserve holdings.

**Q. How could the euro change the dollar's use as an international currency by the private sector?**

A. The dollar is used by the private sector in a variety of ways. The dollar is the primary transaction currency in international trade. Presently, the dollar plays a dominant role in invoicing around the world, especially for primary commodities like oil. In 1998, it was estimated that the dollar served as the payment currency for about 48 percent of world trade, although the U.S. share of world trade was about 18 percent. This provides an incentive for companies engaged in international trade to maintain working balances in dollars. In the EU's view, the use of the euro in trade invoicing (not counting intra-euro area trade) is likely to exceed the sum of the currencies that have been replaced by the euro. This is due in part to economies of scale in the use of currencies leading to lower transaction costs and better availability of hedging instruments.

The dollar is also the primary currency of international banking. Bank for International Settlements (BIS)[13] data show that at the end of 1998, about 41 percent of international bank assets[14] were denominated in U.S. dollars (see fig. 2.1); however, the U.S. banks' share of international bank assets was about 11 percent. This shows that the dollar is used by non-U.S. banks as well as U.S. banks.

---

[13] BIS is an organization of major central banks that is based in Basel, Switzerland. It is the principal forum for consultation, cooperation, and information exchange among central bankers.

[14] International bank assets are assets of banks located in 24 major industrialized countries or off-shore centers.

The dollar's 41-percent share of international bank assets in 1998 was well below its 63-percent share in 1985. At the end of 1998, the largest portion of the "all other currencies" category was the national currencies of euro area members, which accounted for about 31 percent of international bank assets.

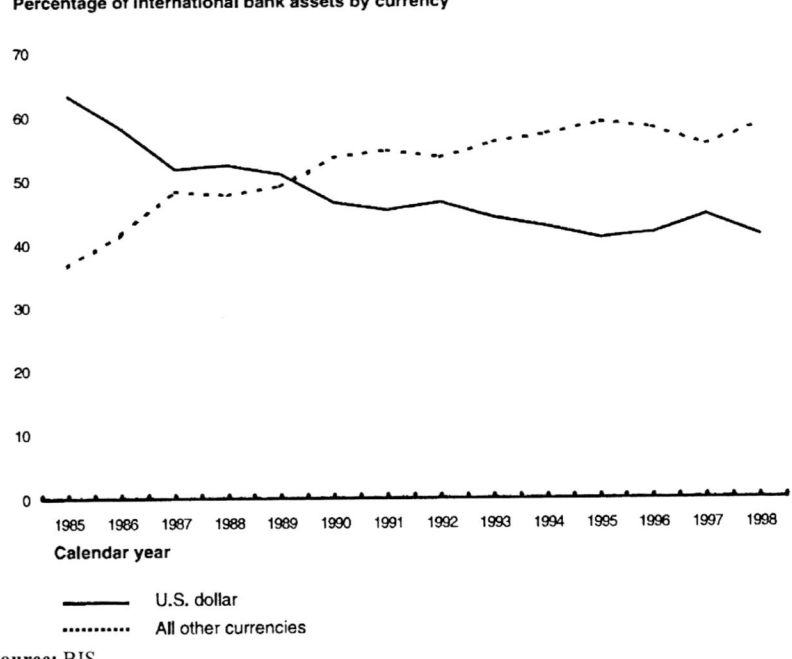

**Figure 2.1:** Cross-Border Assets of Banks in Industrial Countries by Currency (1985-1998)

Source: BIS.

A large share of international bonds and notes is issued in dollars.[15] (See fig. 2.2.) BIS data show that at the end of 1998, about 45 percent of international bonds and notes outstanding was denominated in dollars. Less than half of these have been issued by U.S. borrowers, who accounted for 20 percent of the total outstanding. The largest share of bonds and notes issued

---

[15] International bonds and notes include both domestic currency issues in a given country by nonresidents of that country (e.g., dollar bonds issued in the United States by foreign entities) and foreign currency issues in a given country by either residents or nonresidents (e.g., dollar bonds issued in London by either a U.S. company or a British company).

in currencies other than the dollar was issued in the national currencies of euro area members. These currencies accounted for about 28 percent of the total at the end of 1998. During the period 1985 to 1998, the dollar share of international bonds and notes outstanding fluctuated between a high of about 57 percent in 1985 to a low of about 35 percent in 1995.

**Figure 2.2:** International Bond and Note Issues Outstanding by Currency (1985-1998)

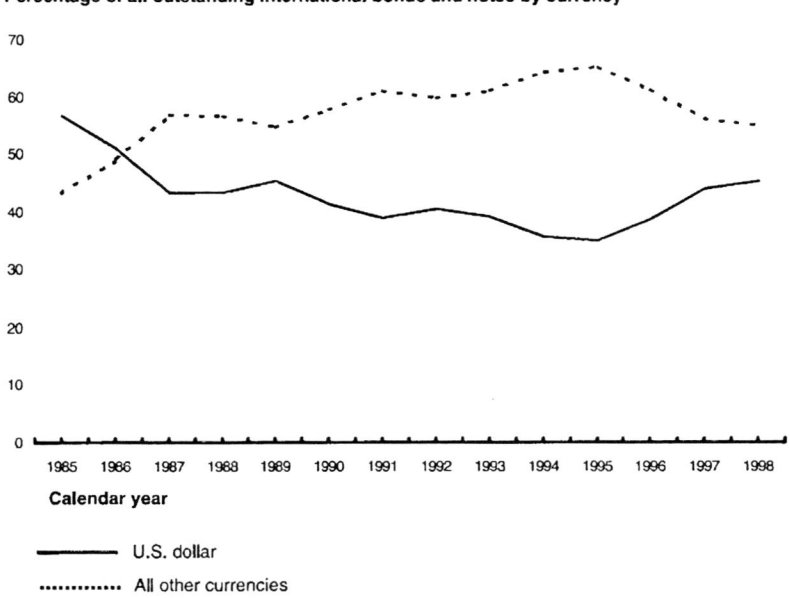

Source: BIS.

In some foreign countries, U.S. dollar currency notes circulate in substantial amounts.[16] In these countries, the dollar is used as a substitute for local cash transactions—particularly in countries where hyperinflation or social disorder undermines the public's faith in the local currency. In mid-1998, it was estimated that about 60 percent of the $441 billion dollar notes in circulation—about $265 billion--were held outside the United States. Many of these dollar notes are used in underground economies, and it is

---

[16] See C. Randall Henning, *Cooperating with Europe's Monetary Union*, Institute for International Economics, Washington, D.C.: May 1997.

widely believed that some of these dollars are used as a medium of illicit exchange.

Holdings of paper currency by the public, whether inside or outside the United States, serve as a form of interest-free financing for the U.S. government. Using an interest rate of 5 percent, the foreign holdings of dollar notes yield a seigniorage of about $13 billion a year. That is, the U.S. government saves $13 billion annually because foreigners hold currency instead of interest-paying bonds. If euros were to become more widely used for similar purposes, outside the euro area there would be a decreased demand for dollars, and it is possible that the U.S. government would lose some earnings it receives through seigniorage. A variety of factors will determine whether the emergence of the euro will have a significant impact on the international role of the dollar. Euro area companies may be in a stronger position than before to require that the euro be used in their transactions in order to avoid exchange rate risk. The analysts we spoke with told us that those nonindustrial countries that had been conducting their cross-border transactions in the currencies of the member countries of the euro area are expected to do so in euros. Those developing countries closely linked to the United States would continue to use dollars.

Over the longer term, several of the analysts we spoke with believe that the comparative status of the dollar and euro as international currencies may be affected by potential developments in the euro area payments and securities settlements infrastructure. The U.S. dollar is supported by systems that allow money and financial assets to be moved with great speed, efficiency, and reliability. In the euro area, each country still has its own separate systems for wholesale payments. The ECB has established a new wholesale system for cross-border euro payments called Trans-European Automated Real-Time Gross Settlement Express Transfer System (TARGET), which links the comparable systems of each member central bank. TARGET must be accessed through the national systems, which are not yet harmonized. Nonetheless, progress is being made in dealing with euro area-wide payments and securities infrastructure. The EU expects lower transaction costs to result from this process. Through the first 10 months of 1999, TARGET carried 69 percent of euro payments value. Moreover, providers of securities infrastructure services announced a wide range of plans involving integration of their systems through links or crossborder alliances. Lower transaction costs are not only related to official payments systems and securities settlement systems, but also to economies of scale for enterprises, banks, and in the foreign exchange markets.

Responses of investment managers to the euro as an investment and financing currency will depend on the euro's competitiveness with the dollar as an international currency.[17] The decisions of these private agents will be influenced by factors that make euro-denominated investments attractive, such as the prospective ECB monetary policy stance, the inflation rate in the euro area, the perceived riskiness of the rate of return on euro-denominated assets, and economic growth in Europe.

Economic size favors neither the dollar nor the euro because the economies are similar in size. Relative confidence in the currencies is likely to depend upon both economic performance and the monetary policy stances taken by the respective central banks. Both the Federal Reserve and the ECB have pursued stable monetary policies aimed at low inflation. Officials in the United States and Europe stressed that the dollar's international role will not be challenged if the underlying strength of the U.S. economy remains fundamentally sound.

It is possible that the euro could eventually affect the dollar's position as the premier international currency. However, most analysts we spoke with and documents we reviewed maintained that the euro is not likely to cause a sudden decline in the dollar's use as an international currency in the near future, and any shift away from the dollar will be gradual. Some experts argue that the euro is not likely to displace the dollar's international role because of inertia in the use of international currencies and that at best, the euro will complement the dollar. There are, however, other experts who argue that the euro will compete with the dollar for a substantial share of its international role. An intermediate view is that the euro's gains will not necessarily come at the expense of the dollar because increased use of the euro may not decrease the use of the dollar in absolute terms.

## Q. How could the euro change the dollar's use as an international currency for official purposes?

A. Central banks around the world hold large amounts of currency reserves, and a large portion of these reserves is denominated in dollars. Central banks hold foreign currency reserves for use in case they wish to intervene in foreign exchange markets to prevent the exchange rate of their domestic currency from falling against foreign currencies.[18] From 1985

---

[17] See "The International Role of the Euro," *ECB Monthly Bulletin*, August 1999.
[18] The foreign exchange markets are where domestic currency is exchanged for foreign currency. When one country experiences an increase in demand for foreign currency relative to its domestic currency, the exchange rate of the domestic currency will fall. A central bank can "intervene" or try to influence this by selling foreign currency and buying its domestic currency.

through 1998, the dollar's share of official foreign exchange reserves ranged between about 44 percent and 57 percent, the peak year being 1998. (See fig. 2.3.) At that time, the euro area national currencies and the European Currency Unit (ECU)[19] accounted for about 15 percent of official currency reserves.

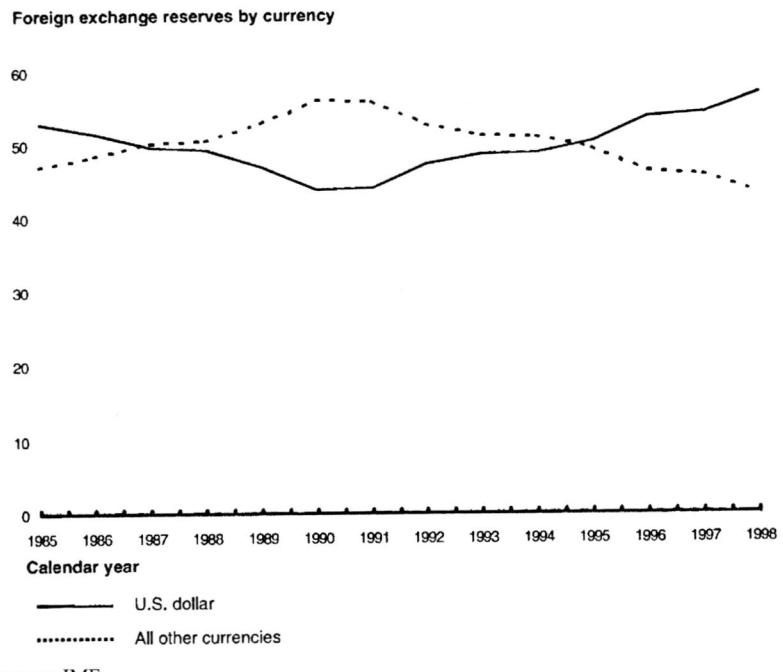

**Figure 2.3:** Official Foreign Exchange Reserves by Currency Denomination (1985-1998)

Source: IMF.

Another official international role for a currency is as a base against which other countries might "peg" their exchange rates. Countries peg their exchange rates by tying the value of their currency to the currency of another country—typically the currency of its largest trading partner. The value of the pegged currency rises or falls simultaneously with the value of the

---

[19] The European Currency Unit is a composite basket of currencies in which each currency is weighted according to its share in intra- European trade, its percentage share of EU gross national product, and the relative importance of each country's foreign exchange reserves. As of January 1, 1999, the ECU was converted into the euro on a one-for-one basis.

currency to which it is tied. Several dozen smaller countries around the world peg their currencies to the dollar, the euro, other currencies, or a basket of currencies. A country that pegs its currency to another is likely to keep most of its foreign exchange reserves in that other currency.

Some Eastern European countries, which have pegged their currencies to the German mark in the past, now peg their currencies to the euro. The euro has replaced the former national currencies of the French franc and the Portuguese escudo as a pegging currency. The EU expects more countries to peg their currencies to the euro in the future, in some cases upon accession to the EU. Experts we spoke with expect the countries that pegged their exchange rates to the dollar before the advent of the euro to continue to do so because it makes economic sense for them.

Most Latin American and Asian countries have closer trade relations with the United States than with Europe, and thus it seems likely that these countries will continue to use the dollar as a reserve currency. However, it also seems likely that the euro would be used by countries that intend to peg their exchange rates to the euro or to intervene in currency markets in the euro for other purposes.

Before the inauguration of the euro, there were questions about whether the European System of Central Banks (ESCB)[20] and other central banks around the world might sell large amounts of their dollar reserves. Prior to EMU, the central banks of the present members of the euro area needed part of their reserves for possible intervention in the currency markets in case of instability between their currencies. Once EMU converted the intrazone trade and capital flows into domestic-currency transactions, such intervention was no longer necessary, and it was thought that the pooled foreign currency reserves of the ESCB might exceed the potential reserve needs of EMU.[21] The ECB reported that in 1999 some of the national central banks did reduce the proportion of foreign reserves in their balance sheets. Nonetheless, such actions were not sizeable; between the end of January and the end of October 1999, the combined foreign exchange reserves of the euro area only dropped from $234 billion to $223 billion. The impact of reduction in excess reserves would be small relative to the stock of U.S. international assets and liabilities. Moreover, statements from both the ECB and the U.S.

---

[20] ESCB comprises the ECB and the central banks of all EU member countries.
[21] Note that the creation of the euro did reduce the ESCB's currency reserves somewhat, because the portion of each national central bank's reserves that had been in other members' currencies was converted into domestic currency upon creation of the euro. In January 1999, the euro area foreign exchange reserves dropped by $32.8 billion, possibly reflecting this effect.

Treasury indicated that dramatic or abrupt changes in the currency reserves of the central banks were unlikely.

A shift in the type of reserves held by developing countries may have more of an effect on the value of the dollar than a shift by industrialized countries. As of March 1999, International Monetary Fund (IMF) data show that developing countries held 58 percent of global foreign currency reserves, and developed countries held 42 percent of global foreign currency reserves. As of the end of 1998, 57 percent of developing country currency reserves was dollars, and 64 percent of developed country currency reserves was dollars.

The ECB expects the euro to inherit the reserve currency roles of the respective euro area former national currencies and to be the second most used international reserve currency. Most analysts maintain that the advent of the euro is not likely to cause a sudden decline in the use of the dollar as a reserve currency in the near future. Central banks have traditionally refrained from abrupt and large changes in the level and composition of their foreign reserves. Over time, official sector preferences for currency use could change, and the euro could eventually replace part of the dollar's role as a reserve currency, but experts we spoke with expect any change to be gradual. As the euro achieves depth and liquidity, over time central bankers may see it as an increasingly desirable currency for diversification purposes. Ultimately, the ability of the euro to become a major reserve currency will depend on the confidence that both foreign central banks and international investors have in it as well as on its usage in international trade and finance.

Although there are certain economic benefits that derive from the public and private international roles of the dollar, the importance of such benefits is uncertain. Some analysts believe that these roles provide, in addition to economic benefits, important political benefits to the United States that are worth maintaining. Other analysts believe the importance of a country's currency has little to do with the wellbeing of its citizens over the long run, as attested by the experience of many successful economies whose currencies do not have major international roles.

## WHAT COULD BE THE EFFECTS OF EMU ON MONETARY POLICY AND ON EXCHANGE RATES?

**Q. What is monetary policy?**

A. Monetary policy is the set of central bank actions that adjust the supply of money and credit conditions in the economy to achieve a set of policy goals. Important monetary policy goals include price stability, economic growth, and keeping output near its potential and, thus, unemployment low. An additional objective is to manage credit conditions to facilitate a smoothly functioning economy. Monetary policy is designed to affect economic variables such as interest rates and the level of output and employment in the short run in ways compatible with long-run policy objectives.

An "easy" monetary policy lowers unemployment and increases output over the short run through faster monetary growth and possibly lower interest rates. However, these effects may not last over the long term, and such a policy also tends to raise the rate of inflation and decrease the value of the currency on international markets. In contrast, a "tight" monetary policy raises interest rates and lowers inflation, possibly at the cost of higher short-term unemployment. Such a policy can also increase the value of the currency on international markets. A tension exists in monetary policy decisions between the desirable goals of low unemployment and low inflation.

**Q. How is monetary policy set and implemented in the euro area?**

A. In the euro area, monetary policy is decided upon and implemented by the European System of Central Banks (ESCB), which consists of the ECB and the central banks of all EU members.[22] The Governing Council of the ECB—composed of the 6-member Executive Board plus 1 representative from each of the 11 euro area member central banks—formulates monetary policy, and the Executive Board implements monetary policy through the national central banks. A central way monetary policy is conducted is through open market operations--the buying and selling of approved securities.[23]

---

[22] The four EU member states that are not part of the euro area have a special status; they are allowed to conduct their national monetary policies and do not take part in decisionmaking nor in implementation of the common euro area monetary policy.

[23] Other tools of monetary policy include setting (1) the interest rate of the Marginal Lending Facility, through which eligible financial institutions may borrow overnight from ESCB; (2) the interest rate in the Deposit Facility, through which ESCB accepts overnight

According to the Maastricht Treaty, the ECB's primary goal is price stability, which the ECB has operationally defined as less than 2 percent per year of inflation in consumer prices. In contrast to the German Bundesbank, the leading European central bank, which had aimed for a specific rate of growth of its money supply, the ECB's stated policy is to be more flexible and consider other indicators in making monetary policy decisions. Specifically, the ECB has set forth a "two-pillar" strategy for conducting monetary policy, which includes (1) a reference value for money supply growth of 4 ½ percent annually in the broadly-defined money supply measure, M3;[24] and (2) a broad-based assessment of the outlook for inflation generally.

A fundamental question surrounding the introduction of the euro was whether the ECB would pursue a relatively strict monetary policy and maintain low inflation over the long run in the face of potential pressures to pursue an easy monetary policy to lessen (short-run) unemployment. Those who raise this question cited several factors including that almost two-thirds of the ECB's Governing Council are representatives of national central banks that have only recently become independent, and more liberal member governments may come into power and pressure the ECB for a more expansionary monetary policy.

In its brief history, the ECB has appeared to be focused on price stability in numerous public statements. To date, inflation has remained modest, generally not exceeding 2 percent per year, and broader measures of the euro money supply have grown moderately, although above the reference value rate.[25] One issue continues to be how the ECB will conduct monetary policy when economic conditions differ significantly among member countries--if, for example, the economies of some countries, but not others, are depressed by external or internal events.

## Q. How could the euro affect monetary policy in the United States?

**A.** Conducting U.S. monetary policy is the responsibility of the Federal Reserve System (the Fed), the central bank of the United States. Congress

---

deposits from eligible financial institutions; and (3) financial institutions' reserve requirements.

[24] The most common measures of money are M1, M2, and M3. M1 is the narrowest measure and includes the most liquid assets-- currency held by the (nonfinanacial institution) public and checking account-type balances at financial institutions. M2 is a broader concept, and includes, for example, certain time deposits. M3 is the broadest measure; in addition to M2, it includes other assets such as large time deposits, and marketable liabilities of financial institutions.

[25] From December 1998 through January 2000, M3 grew almost 6 percent.

has defined the primary objectives of national economic policy as economic growth, a high level of employment, stable prices, and moderate long-term interest rates, and the Fed is required to pursue these goals.[26] As a practical economic matter, tensions can arise in the pursuit of these goals. In general, low inflation has been a clear priority of U.S. monetary policy over the past 15 years.

Open market operations are the principal means of conducting U.S. monetary policy. They are the responsibility of the Federal Open Market Committee, which comprises all 7 members of the Board of Governors of the Fed plus the presidents of each of the 12 (regional) Federal Reserve banks.[27] After considering the current and expected state of the economy and its future prospects, including domestic and foreign economic activity, output, inflation, wage inflation, interest rates, money supply growth, consumer spending, and securities markets, the committee decides upon what it considers an appropriate open market policy for the New York Federal Reserve Bank to implement. Meetings occur eight times a year.

The Board of Governors oversees two other tools of monetary policy. The discount rate— the rate at which banks and other deposit-taking institutions can borrow from their Federal Reserve Banks—is changed from time to time to reinforce open market operations. Reserve requirements—the schedule by which these institutions must keep reserves as cash in their vaults or as deposits in accounts at the Fed—are rarely changed.

Although the Fed determines U.S. monetary policy primarily on the basis of domestic economic conditions, the Federal Reserve also takes international conditions into account insofar as they influence U.S. domestic objectives. For example, increases in the price of oil, an international commodity, can significantly affect the U.S. inflation rate and has influenced U.S. monetary policy. Similarly, following the Russian default in 1998, the Fed started to ease U.S. monetary policy by lowering short-term interest rates in September to offset the downward effect on U.S. economic growth of increasing weakness in foreign economies. Monetary policy does affect exchange rates; however, according to Fed officials, in recent years the Fed has not intervened in the foreign exchange market, except to combat disorderly markets during brief periods.

---

[26] These laws include The Federal Reserve Act of 1913, which established the Federal Reserve System; The Employment Act of 1946; and The Full Employment and Balanced Growth Act of 1978, also known as the Humphrey-Hawkins Act, after its original sponsors.

[27] At any one time only five presidents may vote, one of whom is the head of the New York Federal Reserve Bank.

Although the Fed has a track record of cooperating and coordinating with some of the central banks in the ESCB, it has little experience dealing with the ECB as it is a new institution. Thus, how those interactions will affect U.S. monetary policy is yet to be determined.

**Q. How can exchange rates vary?**

**A.** Exchange rates vary due to a variety of influences—current and expected monetary, fiscal, and structural policies, as well as cyclical and other economic forces. Exchange rate movements can be characterized in terms of longer term trends and shorter term fluctuations around those trends, termed volatility. Generally, the more that two countries' fundamental economic conditions or macroeconomic policies differ, the greater will be the trend movement of their common exchange rate, other things being equal. Volatility reflects market participants' reactions to new information on a variety of changing economic as well as other conditions. Actual or expected intervention by the central banking authority in the foreign exchange market to maintain the exchange rate can, in certain cases, reduce volatility.

**Q. What is the recent history of exchange rate variations among euro area members?**

**A.** Although exchange rates among continental European countries have been relatively stable in recent years, governments have at times experienced difficulties in defending currency values, with the latest currency crisis occurring in 1992-93. Governments of EU member states have tried to lessen exchange rate variability among their countries for some time, due to the high degree of trade and investment among them. Some central banks have intervened in foreign exchange markets and increasingly governments have coordinated macroeconomic policies to reduce exchange rate fluctuations. A common view is that large fluctuations in currency values result in increased costs to businesses to cover the risks of conducting international transactions, although the effect of such costs on trade volume is not clear.

**Q. How could the euro affect exchange rates with other currencies?**

**A.** The euro's effect on the volatility of the euro area's external exchange rate with respect to other currencies—e.g., the dollar—has been subject to debate among international economists. Some economists have argued that the euro will be more volatile against other currencies than were the major national currencies of euro area members, and others have argued that volatility will be less.

Reasons given for higher expected volatility are (1) during the initial period of the euro there will be greater uncertainty about how the ECB will conduct monetary policy, a rapidly changing financial environment in Europe, and unknown shifts by international investors and central banks; and (2) the ECB may be less concerned about exchange rate fluctuation than the individual central banks had been before EMU because creation of the large, single-currency zone reduces the share of GDP that is influenced by these fluctuations.

One reason given for possible lower volatility is that the monetary policy of the euro area is likely to respond to business conditions across the euro area and not a particular country. These conditions can vary across countries. Thus, interest rates in the euro area, reflecting more heterogeneous business conditions, could fluctuate less than they would have for one country, leading to less fluctuation in capital flows between the euro area and the rest of the world, and less fluctuation in the euro exchange rate, other things being equal.

Over the longer term, the credibility of the value of the euro currency will likely depend primarily on the performance of euro area economies and their economic policy mix.

**Q. How has the euro-dollar exchange rate varied?**

**A.** After its introduction in January 1999, the euro steadily declined in value, going from $1.17 to about $1.02 by July 1. Its value recovered somewhat after that but declined again, dropping below $0.98 by the end of January 2000, a more than 16-percent depreciation since January 1999. Because the euro was launched at a point when the values of euro area currencies against the dollar were relatively high compared to the previous 2 years, it is difficult to know at this point the significance of this decline. One factor behind the depreciation against the dollar may be the relative strength of the U.S. economy, which led to an increased demand by foreigners for U.S. stocks and bonds and increased foreign direct investment in the United States. Some analysts also believe that slow progress in restructuring economies in some euro area countries has also lowered the market's confidence in the euro. Figure 3.1 shows recent trends in the dollar-euro area exchange rate.

**Figure 3.1:** Dollar-Euro Area Exchange Rate, January 1996 – February 2000

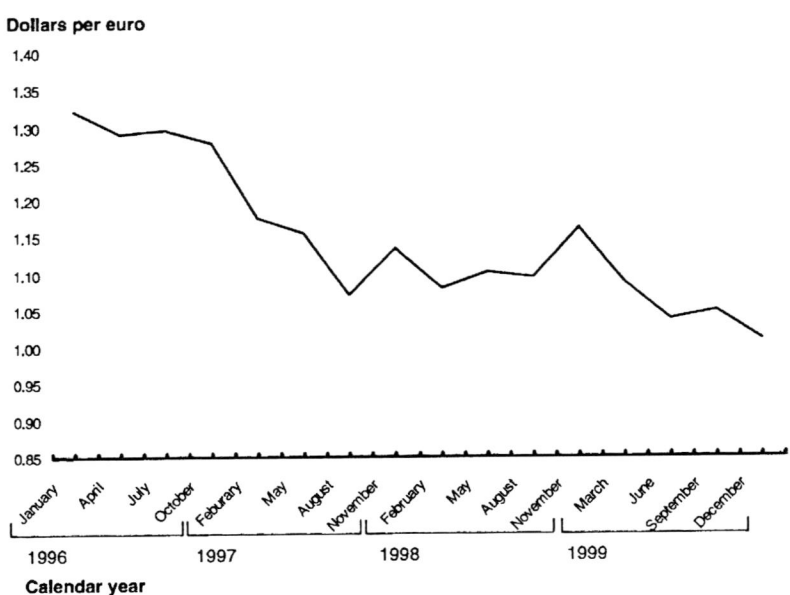

**Note:** Values before January 1999 reflect a synthetic euro based on trade-weighted averages of the exchange rates of the 11 euro area countries. Beginning in January 1999, values reflect observed dollar-euro exchange rates.
**Source:** Department of Commerce.

Future movements of the dollar-euro exchange rate are likely to depend upon the macroeconomic policies of the United States and euro area countries, their future relative economic growth, how quickly euro area countries restructure their economies, and other forces affecting these economies.

# WHAT ARE THE IMPLICATIONS OF EMU FOR FINANCIAL MARKETS, FINANCIAL INSTITUTIONS, AND THEIR REGULATION?

**Q. What are the implications of the European Monetary Union (EMU) for financial markets, institutions, and their regulation?**
  **A.** EMU is a major step in the economic unification of Europe, which began with the Treaty of Rome in 1957. As with the nonfinancial aspects of

unification, EMU is intended to strengthen Europe economically by achieving the benefits of economies of scale. From the U.S. perspective, key questions about EMU focus on financial markets, banking, and financial regulation.

## Q. How could the euro affect financial markets in Europe and the United States?

A. Financial markets serve investors and users of capital better when the markets have sufficient size and liquidity to allow large sums to be traded without destabilizing prices. By substituting a single currency for numerous currencies that could fluctuate against each other, EMU and the euro are intended to add to the depth, liquidity, and competitiveness of capital markets in the euro area, and to lower trading costs for borrowers. Although EMU does not by itself make one uniform and unified market, the establishment of the single currency removes an important impediment to the intra-euro area capital flows: i.e., exchange rate risk. Some experts have said that the largest effect of the creation of the euro will be the transformation of financial services in Europe. They predict that European stock and bond markets will become more integrated over time and could rival stock and bond markets in the United States. The introduction of the euro may eventually create the largest single-currency financial market in the world.[28]

Various structural differences still exist in the euro area financial markets. The development of Europe-wide private securities markets has thus far been inhibited by long-standing regulations for issuing, dealing, and trading securities; by elements of tax systems that encourage bank financing; and by differences in market practices and in securities and settlement systems. With the introduction of the euro, European financial markets could become less segmented and market practices could be more uniform.

Nonetheless, the first year of the euro was marked by a surge of activity in euro-denominated international debt securities. In the first 9 months of 1999, announced new issues of such securities almost doubled compared to the amounts for the pre-EMU currencies in January-September 1998. As shown in figure 4.1, in the 1999 period, the euro-denominated share of international securities issues climbed, and that of dollar-denominated announced issues dropped. The inauguration of the euro was an important factor in the strength of euro-denominated issues: according to BIS, the

---

[28] The market value of bonds, equities, and bank assets issued in EU countries, not euro area countries, amounted to more than $27 billion at the end of 1995. This is larger than the number for North America (See *International Capital Markets: Developments, Prospects, and Key Policy Issues.* IMF, Nov.1997).

merger of euro area currencies can broaden the range of investors who might be interested in investing in some bond issues and also resulted in a pooling of investment demand. One reason for this increased bond issuance in 1999 was an upsurge in merger and acquisition activity in the euro area, according to an IMF official. One financial services industry official told us that part of the surge in euro issues last year may have reflected temporarily favorable terms offered by underwriters competing to establish market share.

**Figure 4.1:** Announced New Issues of International Bonds and Notes (January – September 1998 and 1999)

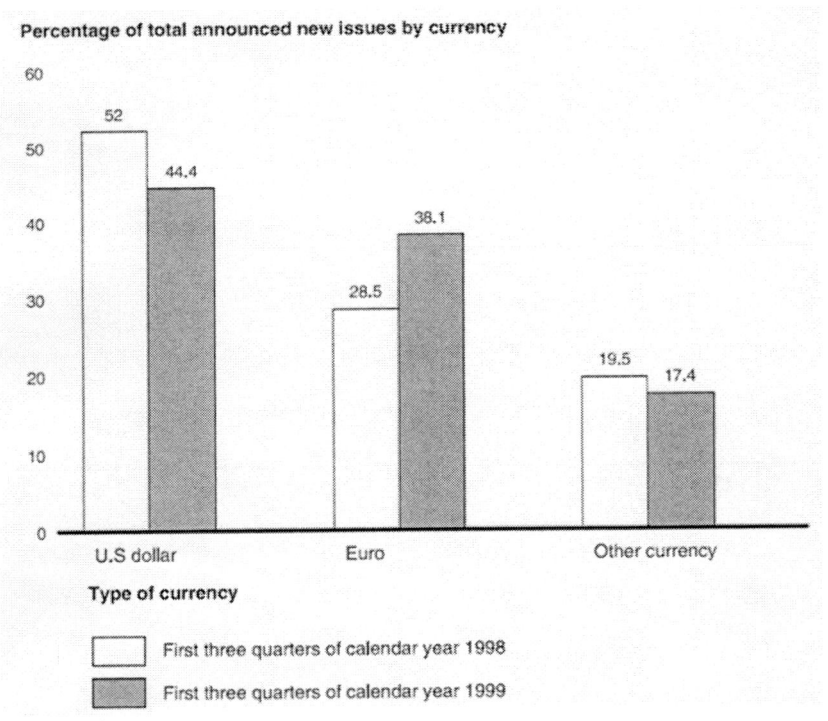

Source: BIS.

Just as dollar-denominated debt issues have been issued by non-U.S. entities, euro-denominated issues have been issued by non-euro area entities. Countries such as Brazil, Argentina, South Africa, and Canada have launched euro issues in significant amounts; according to the ECB, this was in order to rebalance the currency composition of their foreign debt. Moreover, U.S.-based companies have issued euro-denominated debt.

Nonetheless, there is a stronger "home-currency bias" for euro-denominated issues; BIS data show that less than half of outstanding dollar-denominated issues have been issued by U.S. entities, but 68 percent of euro-denominated issuance has been raised by euro area borrowers. Most of the rise in international debt securities issuance in 1999 has come from European companies, a growth that BIS ascribes to the euro.

Not only was there an increase in the total amount of euro-denominated funds raised in 1999, there was also a broadening of the type of European companies that were able to tap this market. Previously, corporate securities issuance in Europe had been primarily by the highest-rated and best-known companies; other companies were more dependent on financing from banks. Changes in investor strategies stemming from the merging of currencies, however, facilitated the entry of lower rated borrowers into the international bond market. Because EMU will permit investors to more accurately assess and price corporate risk, higher yielding debt issued by small to medium sized or highly leveraged companies will become more attractive. The emergence of a European junk bond market is widely predicted.

An opening of securities issuance to less-than-highest-rated companies may lessen some borrowers' dependence on bank loans. This would move Europe toward a more U.S.-style financial system, where financial markets are a more important source of finance than bank lending. Figure 4.2 shows the comparative shares of securities and bank financing in the euro area countries and the United States in 1995. In the United States, combined stock market capitalization plus outstanding debt securities amounted to $17.9 trillion, compared to bank assets of $5 trillion.[29] In the euro area countries, the comparative sizes were reversed, with bank assets of $12 trillion exceeding combined stock and debt securities of $9 trillion.

The faster growth of euro-denominated activity on the international financial markets does not appear to have been at the expense of U.S. entities. As noted, U.S.-based borrowers have issued euro-denominated debt. Moreover, the move toward a more unified financial market in the euro area has presented opportunities for U.S. financial services companies. These companies, through their experience at home, have developed considerable expertise in such activities as securities underwriting and mergers and acquisitions. Notwithstanding shifts in the currency composition of issues in 1999, data for the first 9 months of 1999 show that U.S. investment banks increased their share of international bond underwriting to 45 percent, up

---

[29] Market capitalization is the value of outstanding shares of securities listed on exchanges. It is calculated by multiplying share price by number of outstanding shares.

from 41 percent in 1998. European underwriters had about a 40-percent share in the 1999 period.

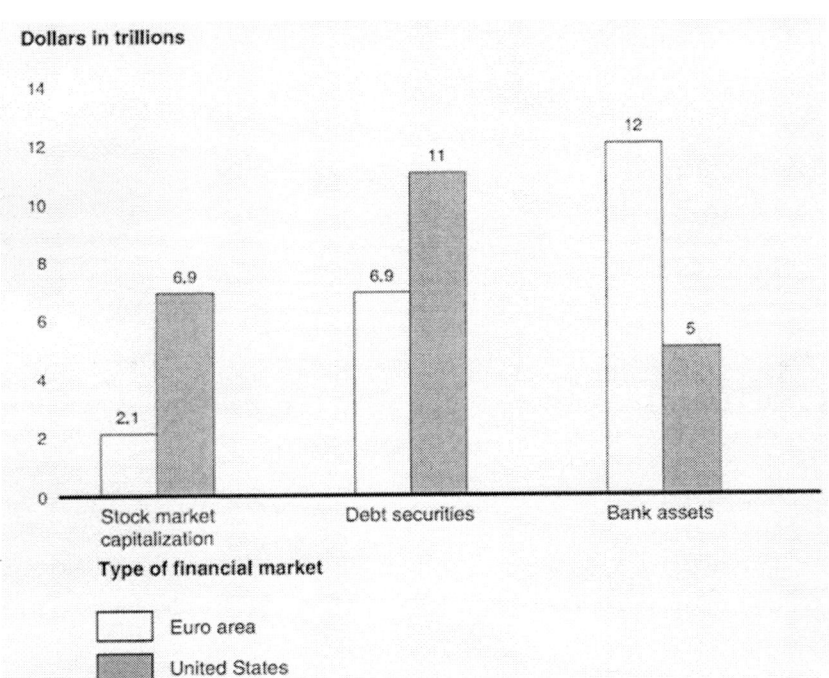

Figure 4.2: Size of Euro Area Versus United States Financial Markets (End- 1995)

Source: IMF.

**Q. What impact might the euro have on the market for U.S. Treasuries?**

A. By eliminating currency risk on cross-border transactions, the introduction of the euro has reduced the cost of issuing and investing in euro area government securities. Some analysts have questioned whether the U.S. Treasury bond market might be challenged by a euro-denominated government bond market of bonds issued by euro area countries—especially in an era when the United States is issuing less debt. This question arises because existing euro area national government debts that were previously denominated in national currencies and all future issues are now denominated in the single currency. The totals of euro area government debt exceed the amount of publicly issued U.S. Treasury debt.

Nonetheless, since the conversion of government debt to the euro, interest rate differentials still exist between the different governments' debt. One analyst has compared these interest rate differentials to the different interest rates of U.S. state and municipal bonds. Although there has been some convergence of interest rates, these differentials reflect, among other things, the respective credit standing of each government's debt, which still depends on that country's ability to service its debts in the future. There is no common taxing authority in the euro area and no statutory guarantees of one country's debt by another. Each euro area member has different financial needs, fiscal policies, and regulations. Interest rate differentials may also depend on issuing techniques, clearance and settlement procedures, and legal procedures. Thus, the government bonds are not deemed to be fungible, and there are still as many different government bond markets as there had been previously. Treasury officials we spoke with believe that the possibility of a unified euro-government bond market competing with the U.S. Treasury market is unlikely at the present time.

According to the EU, although the euro area government bond market is not yet unified, greater harmonization is being promoted through extensive consultations that take place among national debt offices on instruments and issuing techniques and practices. A European debt agency has been proposed to issue debt instruments on behalf of national governments. Such a supranational debt agency would require a costly process of revision and amendment of European treaties.

## Q. How could the euro affect banking in Europe and the United States?

A. Banks operating in the euro area, including U.S. banks, are facing a number of possible effects stemming from the establishment of EMU.[30] The reduction of foreign exchange activity in currencies replaced by the euro was regarded by banks as the main negative consequence of EMU. Creation of a single-currency area removes one deterrent to banks in any one euro area country from conducting banking in another euro area country, namely the risk of adverse moves of exchange rates. Because the disappearance of national currencies reduces the home currency advantages that banks in euro area countries had vis-à-vis banks in other euro area countries, the introduction of the euro can be expected to trigger a further increase in cross-

---

[30] Other fundamental forces have also led to changes in the financial system, including financial liberalization, innovation, technological progress, and diversification of savings and investment portfolios.

border competition and operations of banks. This increased competition could put downward pressure on profitability.

Faced with the potential for greater competition and the need to increase efficiency and reduce costs, banks in the euro area countries have embarked on a wave of mergers and acquisitions in an attempt to enhance their size and competitiveness. In terms of the nominal value of deals, bank mergers in the euro area surpassed those of the United States by some 70 percent in 1999. Thus far, however, consolidation activity has mostly been within national borders, in part because national authorities have appeared reluctant to approve major foreign ownership roles in their domestic banking systems. That is, although the market shares of foreign institutions have recently shown a gradual increase in a number of countries, the euro area banking sector is still fragmented along national lines. The need to become familiar with conditions in the various national markets and the difficulty of developing pan-European banking products have constituted barriers to cross-border banking activity. In addition, the EU believes there are sound economic and practical reasons, such as language differences, for consolidation taking place first on a national level.

All banks operating in the euro area, as well as banks in London and elsewhere, that had accounts in euro area national currencies report that they have had to expend substantial sums adding new systems for recording and managing activities in the new currency. Moreover, banks' earnings may be reduced by the disappearance, culminating in 2002, of revenues generated from customers' foreign exchange trading between the national currencies.

In addition, there could be a more fundamental adjustment of banks' role in financing in the euro area in the future. As shown in figure 4.2, the euro area's financial markets are dominated by bank financing, followed by debt security financing, with stock markets least important. In contrast, the financial markets in the United States are dominated by debt securities financing, followed by stock market financing, with bank financing least important.

As noted in the above discussion of financial markets, EMU is expected by many experts to bolster the capacity and efficiency of euro area capital markets. This development would allow a broader spectrum of euro area companies to raise money by issuing securities, making the companies less dependent on borrowing from banks. According to the EU, corporate bond issuance in euro in 1999 was about four times as great as bond issuance in euro area member national currencies in 1998.

Furthermore, retail banks in most euro area countries are relatively inefficient. Financial systems in Europe are "over-banked" in that complex ownership structures have prevented exit and entry, retarded innovation, and perpetrated mispricing of financial services.[31] The introduction of the single currency is thought likely to accelerate the transformation of European finance by eliminating home currency advantages that EU banks have had in their local deposit-taking and lending activities.

The impact of these developments on U.S. banks would vary with the business focus of each bank. All U.S. banks operating in Europe presumably faced extra costs from upgrading their accounts and management systems to accommodate the euro. But the disappearance of revenues from foreign exchange trading among national currencies would affect only those banks active in this business. Similarly, the possibility that some groups of companies will be able to raise money by issuing securities, thus borrowing less from their banks, would not necessarily affect all U.S. banks operating in Europe, only those that have been lending to these groups of companies. On a broader level, however, if subsequent mergers in Europe eventually lead to stronger, more efficient financial institutions, U.S. banks would face increased competition. This would affect U.S. banks doing business in Europe; and it could also make some larger European banks more formidable competitors worldwide, including in the U.S. market itself.

**Q. How could the euro affect the regulation of financial services companies in the United States and Europe?**

A. Monetary union in Europe does not mean that new financial regulatory and supervisory structures have been created. Creation of the ECB did not entail any transfer of supervisory powers to the ECB. Euro area countries continue to regulate financial services at the national level supplemented by EU directives.[32] At the national level there are a variety of regulatory arrangements. In some cases, bank supervisory functions are combined with monetary policy functions within the central bank. Other countries assign supervisory responsibility to another agency. There are considerable differences in the regulation of bank activities and their ownership structure across EU countries. Other nonharmonized regulatory differences include taxation, subsidies, supervisory reporting, on-site

---

[31] See Folkerts-Landau, David, D.J. Mathieson, and G.J. Schinasi. "EMU: Systemic Implications and Challenges," *International Capital Markets: Developments, Prospects, and Key Policy Issues.* Washington, D.C.: IMF, Nov. 1997.

[32] Directives are measures passed by the European Commission that EU member national governments are required to adopt through their own national legislation. Current EU directives allow freedom of establishment of cross-border service provision and have substantially harmonized prudential regulation, including solvency ratios and large exposures.

inspections, provisions for bank liquidation and restructuring of banks, and other factors. Unless further harmonization takes place, banking regulations will continue to grant considerably different powers to banks in each country.

One important restriction on intra-euro area cross-border investment has been made irrelevant by the euro. The EU has a matching rule that liabilities in a foreign currency must be 80-percent matched by assets in the same currency. That is, fund managers must invest in assets denominated in the same currencies as the liabilities they back. This rule applies to investments of pension funds and insurance companies. With the advent of EMU, insurance companies will be able to invest their assets in any country of the euro area as long as their liabilities are denominated in euros. Asset allocation will move away from domestic equities and bonds to those from all EMU participant countries.

The implementation of several EU directives and the Basel Accord on capital adequacy[33] have not fully harmonized capital standards. The EU is currently conducting a review of its capital adequacy standards. In the meantime, capital standards differ somewhat across EU countries owing to the different lists of items that banks can use to meet capital requirements. Likewise, supervisory practices vary in terms of procedures for examinations and inspections, disclosure of regulatory reporting, lending limits, and limits on bank activities abroad.

One important issue has been ambiguity about mechanisms for resolving banking crises. The Maastricht Treaty is silent about lender of last resort responsibilities. There is no central authority with the explicit mandate to ensure market stability over the EMU financial system. Situations could arise in which the ECB would have to act decisively and quickly. The euro area central banks, the ECB, and bank supervisors would have to cooperate and share information. According to the EU, the ECB has made it clear that it is satisfied with the organization of lender of last resort activities. However, work remains to be done in the area of crisis management involving central banks, supervisory organizations, and Ministers of Finance.

Although there is an EU requirement for all EU countries to develop deposit insurance systems, the structure of deposit insurance is far from harmonized. Deposit insurance administration is the responsibility of the government in five EU countries, of the banking system in six, and of both in the remaining four. Funding is to be provided before the occurrence of a

---

[33] The Basel Accord, developed under the auspices of BIS, is a riskbased capital standards framework for internationally active banks.

bank failure in 10 of the 15 EU countries and after the occurrence of a failure in the remaining countries. Deposit insurance premiums are risk-based only in two euro area countries, and the basis on which the premium is calculated varies considerably across the EU. The extent of coverage is uneven ranging from a low of $12,000 in one country to full coverage in another euro area country. This lack of harmonization could be a concern for regulators if it triggers regulatory competition between national banking systems with funds flowing towards countries offering the most protection.

## WHAT ARE THE IMPLICATIONS OF THE EURO FOR U.S. TRADE AND INVESTMENT WITH EUROPE?

**Q. What are the current levels and composition of trade between the United States and the EU?**

A. The amount of U.S. trade with euro area countries has grown rapidly in recent years. (See fig. 5.1.) In 1998, euro area countries were the second largest U.S. trading partner, behind Canada, accounting for 15 percent of U.S. trade. Although the United States has in recent years had a trade deficit with the euro area countries in terms of merchandise (goods) trade, the service sector has seen a surplus. (See fig. 5.2.)

Germany is the United States' largest trading partner among euro area countries, followed by France and Italy. The composition of U.S. trade with euro area countries, by sector, is similar to that of overall U.S. trade. Among nine aggregate sectoral groupings, trade in the top two accounted for about 60 percent of all U.S.-euro area trade. These top categories are machinery and transport equipment, followed by chemicals and related products. (See fig. 5.3.)

**Figure 5.1:** U.S. Merchandise Trade With Euro Area Countries (1994-1998)

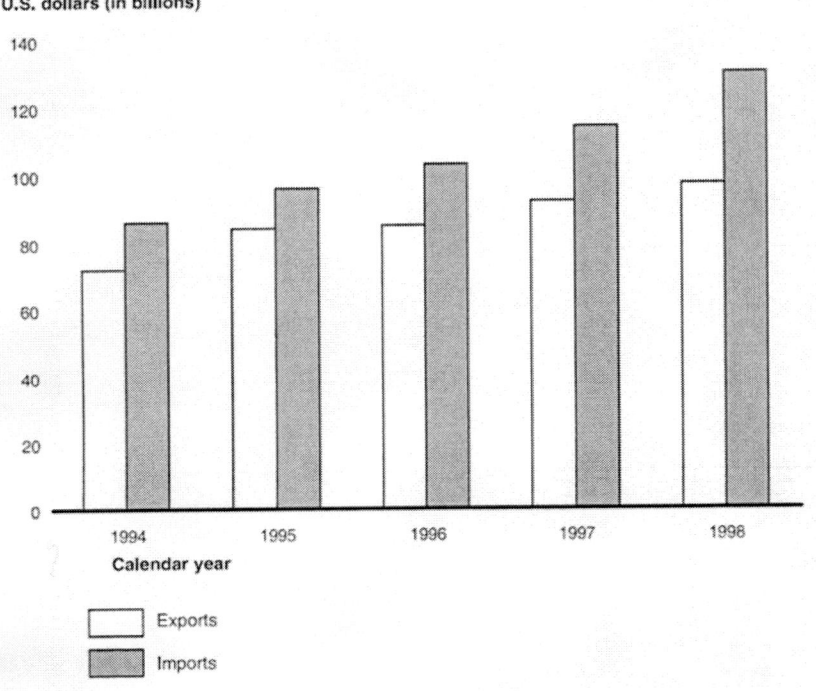

Source: U.S. Department of Commerce.

**Figure 5.2:** U.S. Service Trade With Euro Area Countries (1994-1998)

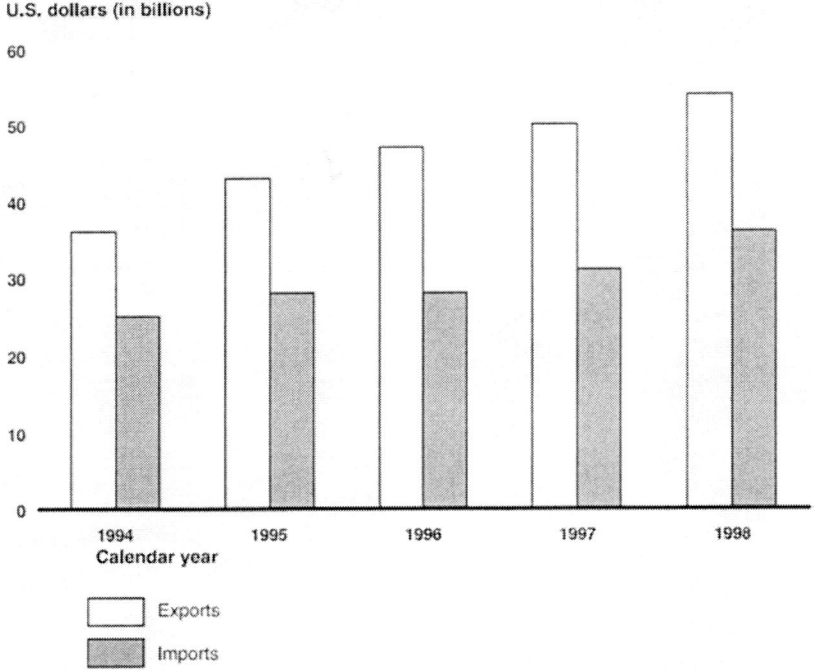

Note: Estimated service trade data are for 13 countries. These data include U.S. service trade with Greece and Denmark in addition to the 11 euro area countries. Thus, these data may overstate to some extent the amount of U.S. service trade with euro area countries.
Source: U.S. Department of Commerce.

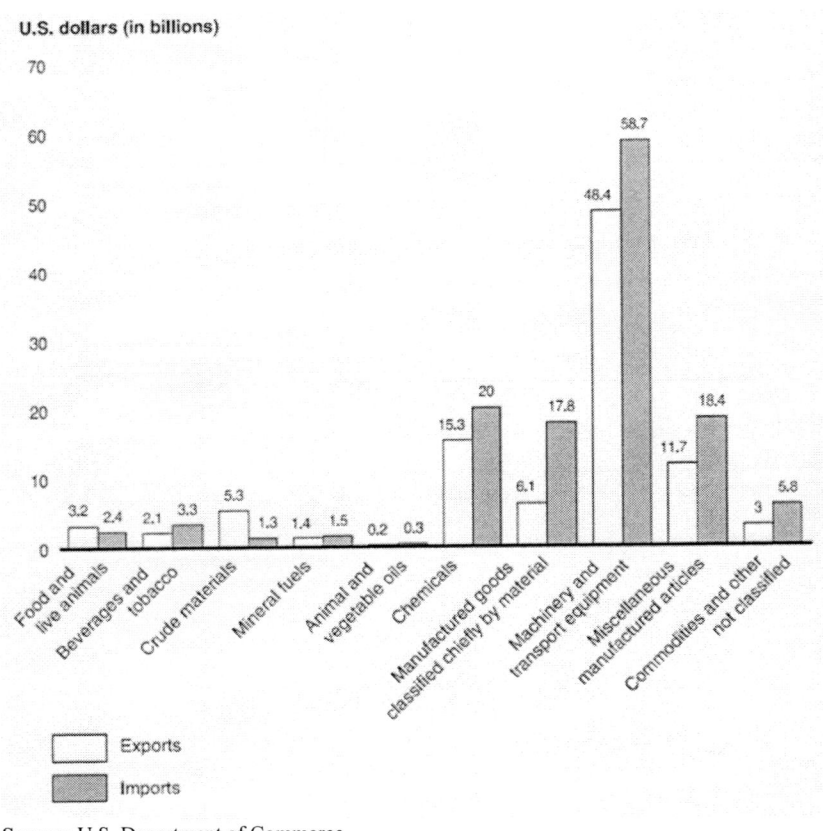

**Figure 5.3:** Composition of U.S. Merchandise Trade with the Euro Area by Sector, 1998

Source: U.S. Department of Commerce.

## Q. How could the euro affect U.S. trade?

A. The introduction of the euro is not expected to have a significant direct impact on U.S. trade with the euro area or with the rest of the world. However, it may indirectly affect future U.S. international trade if it affects the economic growth of the euro area or its competitiveness. If euro area economies grow faster due to the introduction of the single currency, Europe's demand for U.S. exports could rise. That effect could, however, be offset to some degree if the euro leads to European producers becoming more efficient, and thus more competitive in international markets. Both of these effects, however, could be dampened by corresponding exchange rate adjustments between the euro and other currencies.

In addition, the euro could potentially affect the relative attractiveness of U.S. exports to non-European markets if European producers competing with U.S. exporters in those markets become more efficient producers.

Although the overall trade effects are generally believed to be small relative to overall U.S. trade, those business sectors in which U.S. trade with Europe—or U.S. firms' competition with European producers in third-party markets—is concentrated could see more significant impacts.

**Q. How could the euro affect economic growth in Europe?**

**A.** EMU and the euro's effects on economic growth in Europe will not be known for some time because they depend largely on economic policy decisions to be made in the years ahead. On the positive side, a common currency may to some extent reduce costs of doing business. More transparent pricing can enhance competition. These factors can benefit economic growth. In addition, EMU's requirements for fiscal discipline, e.g., low budget deficit and debt levels, should also benefit economic performance over the long run. However, a successful EMU will require a sustained commitment to making what are likely to be difficult policy choices. Because national governments will no longer be able to use monetary or exchange rate policies to adjust to economic downturns, and the use of fiscal policy will be constrained, they will have to turn to structural reforms to allow labor and capital to more easily move among firms, industries, and member countries. According to some analysts, this is how EMU may ultimately provide a strong boost to growth.

However, some analysts continue to express concerns about member countries' and the ECB's ability to make policy choices that are crucial to the euro's long-term success. These include concerns about the countries' ability to keep deficits low; the ECB's ability to maintain price stability; and the countries' ability to, in fact, achieve needed structural reforms.

**Q. What are the recent levels and composition of foreign direct investment (FDI) between the United States and euro area countries?**

**A.** U.S. direct investment in the euro area accounted for about 25 percent of total U.S. FDI at the end of 1998. This share has been fairly stable over the past 3 years. The euro area's direct investment in the United States was about 38 percent of all FDI into the United States at the end of 1998, up from 35 percent in 1997. Europe as a whole accounted for about 67 percent of the total stock of FDI in the United States at the end of 1998.

In recent years, the United States has invested more in the Netherlands, Germany, and France than in other euro area countries, and these three countries also invested more in the United States. (See fig. 5.4.)

**Figure 5.4:** U.S. Direct Investment Position in Euro Area Countries 1998 – Historical Cost Basis Data

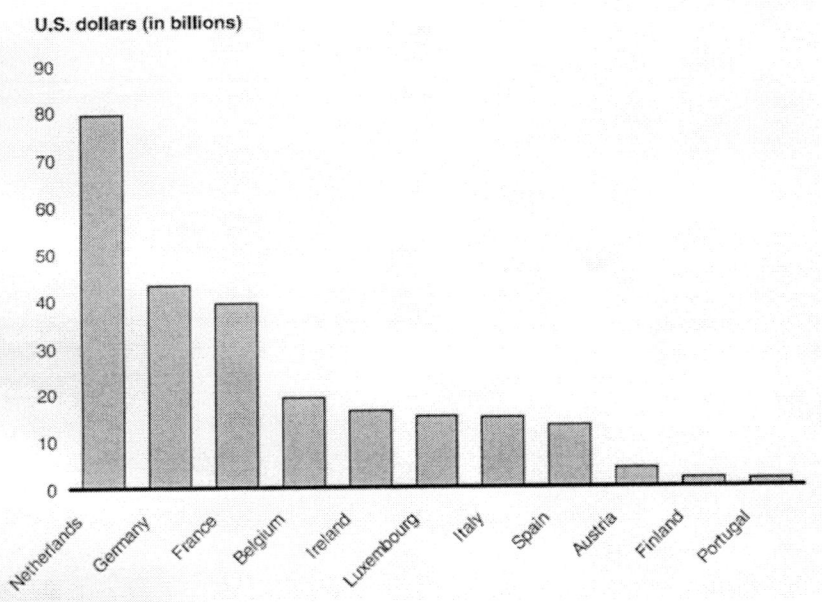

Source: U.S. Department of Commerce.

U.S. companies invested in sectors in euro area countries similar to those that U.S. companies invested in elsewhere: two major groupings (manufacturing sectors and finance/ insurance/ and real estate sectors) each accounted for more than one-third of total direct investment. However, in 1998, the manufacturing sector's share is higher in the euro area than in U.S. FDI elsewhere (39 percent in the euro area compared to 31 percent in all countries). (See fig. 5.5.)

**Figure 5.5:** Sectoral Composition of U.S. Direct Investment Position in Euro Area 1998 – Historical Cost Basis Data

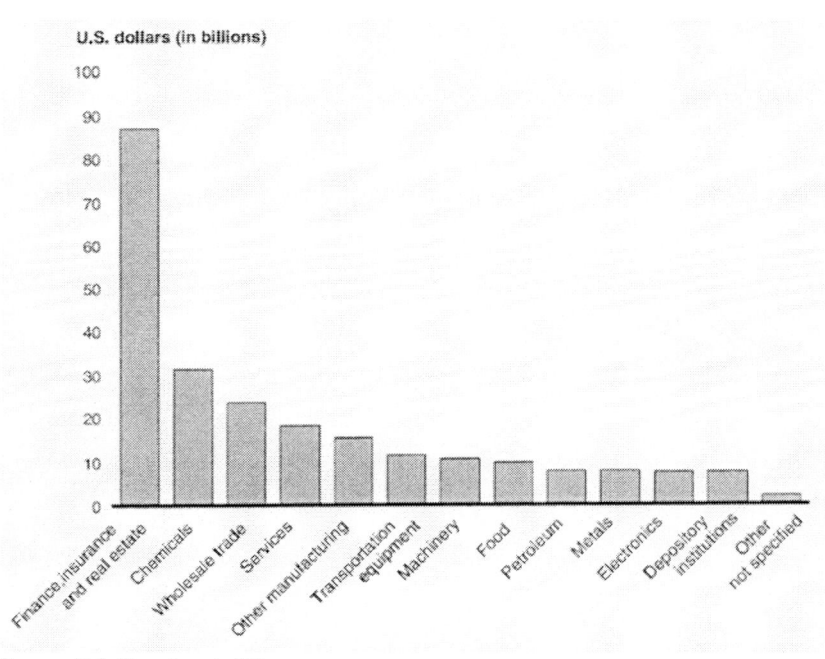

Source: U.S. Department of Commerce.

**Q. How could the euro affect foreign direct investment between the United States and Europe?**

**A.** Euro area countries are more significant partners with the United States in terms of direct foreign investment than in terms of trade. As European economic integration continues, analysts expect countries to remove restrictions on FDI and harmonize regulations over time. This would help all multinationals, including U.S. companies, to consolidate their capacity across Europe and become more cost-efficient. These efficiencies can in part be achieved through mergers. However, at this time it would be quite difficult to predict the magnitude of these impacts and identify the sectors most likely affected. In general, if the euro area economies manage to become more market-oriented with less burdensome government regulation and intervention over time, FDI from many countries could increase, including investment from U.S. companies. Without increased efficiencies, FDI in Europe could well decrease.

# What Are the Implications of EMU for International Economic Policymaking?

**Q. How could EMU directly affect international economic policymaking?**

**A.** The introduction of the euro and the related establishment of the ECB slightly complicate, but do not significantly change, international economic policymaking, according to experts. International economic policy making was, prior to the creation of the ECB, and still is largely the purview of nation states and international organizations composed of representatives from nation states. The ECB is a new, transnational player in these discussions, requiring some new arrangements.

The management of international macroeconomic policy is currently addressed at meetings of the G-7 countries. The seven countries in the G-7 regularly consult on general economic and financial matters.[34]

With the existence of the euro, when the finance ministers from the G-7 meet, the agenda is to be split into two parts. The first part deals with global macroeconomic and exchange rate issues. The president of the ECB and the finance minister from the European country that currently holds the EU presidency is to attend these discussions. Central bank representatives from France, Italy, and Germany do not participate except when one of those countries holds the EU presidency. The second part of the agenda is to deal with such issues as banking regulation, debt relief, and assistance issues. Central bank representatives from France, Italy, and Germany are to participate, but the ECB does not. In addition, the European Commission participates in the second part for discussions on Russia.

Some experts believe that the creation of a more economically unified EU could affect trade negotiations between the United States and the EU. However, U.S. officials told us that they did not expect EMU to affect trade negotiations. These officials told us that the EU took a strong, unified position on trade issues prior to the creation of the euro, and they expect that to continue.

---

[34] The G-7 comprises Canada, France, Germany, Italy, Japan, the United Kingdom, and the United States.

**Q. How could EMU affect decisionmaking
by international financial institutions?**
A. In general, the adoption of the euro and continued evolution of EMU has not had significant effects on the formal decision-making processes of international financial institutions.

EU countries remain individual members of the IMF. Because the IMF grants membership only to countries, the euro area cannot be represented as a single entity on the Executive Board. However, the IMF has granted the ECB observer status at selected Executive Board meetings. In addition, the IMF holds discussions with the ECB and the European Commission as part of its regular economic reporting on its members. The details of this process, known as Article IV consultations, continue to evolve as the IMF tries to ensure that the positions of the ECB, the EU, and national governments are included in assessments of countries in the euro area. The IMF also has changed the composition of its currency, the special drawing rights (SDR), replacing the French franc and the German mark with the euro.[35]

The World Bank and the Organization for Economic Cooperation and Development (OECD) grant membership only to countries, not organizations. Thus, no changes are necessary for the decision-making processes of these organizations. The EU already has a seat on the European Bank for Reconstruction and Development's (EBRD) Board of Directors. The existence of EMU will not change this.

The Bank for International Settlements (BIS), which is owned and controlled by central banks, provides a number of specialized services to them and, through them, to the international financial system more generally. The central banks of 14 EU members hold shares in the BIS. The ECB was invited to become a BIS member in November 1999. According to BIS, formal membership of the ECB will be made final when certain formalities have been completed.

**Q. What are the broader implications of
EMU for global economic policymaking?**
A. If EMU works as European leaders hope, it could lead to an economically stronger and more politically unified Europe. These changes could translate into greater power and influence on the global economic scene. However, experts believe it is too early to discern the extent to which this is taking place. In the near term, most experts believe that

---

[35] The SDR is an international reserve asset created by the IMF from a basket of international currencies.

representatives from national governments will continue to play the predominant roles in international economic policymaking.

# APPENDIX I. OBJECTIVES, SCOPE, AND METHODOLOGY

At the request of the Chairman of the Subcommittee on Domestic and International Monetary Policy of the House Banking Committee, we undertook a review of the implications of Europe's new single currency for the United States. Specifically, our objectives were to answer the following questions: (1) What is the euro and why is Europe moving to it now? (2) What are the potential effects of the euro on the dollar? (3) What are the potential monetary policy and exchange rate effects of the euro? (4) What are the implications of the euro for financial markets and institutions and their regulation? (5) What are the euro's implications for U.S. trade and investment with Europe? And (6) What are the implications of the euro for international economic policymaking?

To meet our objectives, we interviewed officials from the Board of Governors of the Federal Reserve; the Federal Reserve Bank of New York; the Departments of State, Commerce, and the Treasury; the European Commission Delegation to the United States; the IMF; and commercial and investment banks. We also interviewed financial analysts and experts.

In addition, we reviewed U.S. government, EU, ECB, international organization, trade association, academic, industry, and private firm documents, including regulations, annual and other published reports, papers and articles, industry journals, and information available at various sites on the World Wide Web.

We conducted our work in Washington, D.C.; and New York, NY, between November 1999 and January 2000 in accordance with generally accepted government auditing standards.

We requested comments on the technical accuracy of this report from officials at the Departments of State, Commerce, and the Treasury; the Board of Governors of the Federal Reserve; the European Commission Delegation to the United States; and the IMF. Their comments have been incorporated where appropriate.

# APPENDIX II. GLOSSARY

## Bond

Interest-bearing or discounted certificate of indebtedness, paying a fixed rate of interest over the life of the obligation. The issuer is obligated by a written agreement to pay the holder a specific sum of money, usually semiannually but sometimes at maturity, and the face value of the certificate at maturity. Also called fixed-income security.

## Council of the European Union

The Council is composed of ministers of EU governments and represents member states within the EU meeting to discuss specific interests. For example, the Ecofin Council consists of the economic and finance ministers. The Council has decision-making powers in the EU legislative process and coordinates the general economic policy of member states. The Council of the European Union should not be confused with the European Council.

## Economic and Monetary Union

EMU is a three-stage process that was launched in 1990. The first stage lifted restrictions on movements of capital across internal EU borders (July 1990). The second stage set up the European Monetary Institute (EMI) to pave the way for the European Central Bank (ECB) (January 1994). The third stage (January 1999) was the introduction of the euro and beginning of the ECB.

## Euro

The official name for the single currency of 11 of the European Union's 15 countries. The euro was approved at the EU Madrid Summit in December 1995 and went into effect on January 1, 1999.

## Euro Area

The area in which the euro operates as the official single currency. Also called the eurozone and euroland.

## European Central Bank

The ECB is the common, independent central bank for the euro area. The primary objective of the ECB is the maintenance of price stability. The Governing Council of the ECB comprises representatives from the 11 countries in the euro area and formulates the common monetary policy for these countries. The ECB's Executive Board implements monetary policy for the euro area. The General Council has representatives from all 15 countries in the EU and is responsible for a variety of tasks including collecting statistical information and preparing reports and financial statements. The ECB was inaugurated on June 30, 1998, and became operational on January 1, 1999.

## European Commission

The executive body of the European Union. The Commission initiates legislation through proposals and recommendations to the Council of the European Union and European Parliament. The Commission also executes adopted legislation and is the guarantor of the EU Treaty.

## European Council

The European Council comprises the heads of state or government of EU members. The European Council provides the EU with general political guidance. It makes, in practice, major political decisions at its twice yearly summits. The European Council should not be confused with the Council of the European Union.

## European Currency Unit

The European Currency Unit was a composite basket of currencies in which each currency is weighted according to its share in intra-European trade, its percentage share of EU gross national product, and the relative importance of each country's foreign exchange reserves. The monetary unit was created in 1979 by nine European nations to promote currency stability in the European Economic Community. As of Jan. 1, 1999, the ECU was converted into the euro on a one-for-one basis.

## European Monetary Institute

The precursor to the ECB. EMI was formed in January 1994 to advise on monetary issues in the run up to the establishment of EMU.

## European System of Central Banks

The European System of Central Banks is composed of the central banks of the EU countries and the European Central Bank. The ESCB defines and implements monetary policy in the euro area, conducts foreign exchange operations, and manages the official reserves of members states. EU members that are not in the euro area are still part of the ESCB, but do not participate in decisions or implementation of monetary policy. ESCB has full constitutional independence in that it is not permitted to seek or take instructions from European Community institutions or bodies or others.

## European Union

The EU is a treaty-based, supranational organization that defines and manages economic and political cooperation among 15 member countries. The EU attempts to create an ever-closer union by exercising sovereignty voluntarily ceded by its members in economic and political affairs. The European Union replaces the European Community, which succeeds the European Economic Community founded by the Treaty of Rome in 1957.

## Exchange Rate Mechanism

ERM fixed participating member currencies within a band that includes either side of a fixed bilateral central rate against the currencies of other members.

## Exchange Rate Risk

The possibility that the value of a foreign currency will move in an adverse manner due to unforeseen changes in foreign currency exchange rates.

## Foreign Direct Investment

FDI occurs when citizens of one nation purchase assets in some other nation that give them some managerial influence in economic activities related to those assets.

## Foreign Exchange Market

The international market in which currencies are traded. Transactions in foreign exchange include those in the spot, forward, swap, options, and futures markets.

## Foreign Exchange Reserves

The stock of official assets denominated in foreign currencies held by the monetary authorities (finance ministry or central bank) of a country. Reserves enable the monetary authorities to intervene in foreign exchange markets to affect the exchange value of their domestic currency in the market. Reserves are typically part of the balance sheet of the central bank and are managed by the central bank. Reserves are generally invested in low-risk and liquid assets—often in foreign government securities.

## Foreign Portfolio Investment

The purchase by one country's private citizens or their agents of a marketable noncontrolling position in foreign equity and debt securities issues by another country's private citizens, corporation, banks, and governments.

## International Bond

Domestic currency issues in a given country by nonresidents and foreign currency issues in a given country by either residents or nonresidents.

## Maastricht Treaty

The Treaty of European Union agreed at Maastricht, the Netherlands, in 1991, which set out the current procedures and timetable for EMU. The Maastricht Treaty also addressed political integration through provisions on the two areas of security and foreign affairs, and justice and home affairs.

## Market Capitalization

A financial measure calculated by multiplying the number of shares by the market value of shares.

## Monetary Policy

Central bank activity designed to influence the cost and availability of credit. In the United States, the legislated goals of monetary policy are economic growth, full employment, price stability, and balanced trade with other countries. In the euro area, the primary goal is price stability.

## Note

Written promise to pay a specified amount to a certain entity on demand or on a specified date.

## Reserve Currency

Any currency that is commonly used by central banks as part of their foreign exchange reserves. See the definition of foreign exchange reserves.

## Securitization

The broad process whereby capital financing occurs through securities issuance rather than bank financing, including conversion of bank loans and other assets into marketable securities for sale to investors.

## Seigniorage

The profit a government earns from issuing currency notes. Because currency does not pay interest, the issuing government in effect obtains an interest-free loan.

## Trans-European Automated Real-time Gross Settlement Express Transfer (TARGET)

The settlement system for the euro that processes cross-border transactions denominated in euros. It links the national settlement systems of the participating euro area countries and facilitates the borrowing and lending of funds from their central banks.

## APPENDIX III. BIBLIOGRAPHY

Adams, Charles; D. Mathieson; and G. Schinasi. "Progress With European Monetary Integration," *International Capital Markets: Developments, Prospects, and Key Policy Issues*. Washington, D.C.: IMF, Sep. 1999.

Adams, C., et al. "Selected Issues in Mature Financial Systems: EMU, Banking System Performance, and Supervision and Regulation," *International Capital Markets: Developments, Prospects, and Key Policy Issues*. Washington, D.C.: IMF, Sep. 1998.

Bergsten, C. Fred. "The Dollar and the Euro," *Foreign Affairs* Vol. 76, No, 4, Jul./Aug. 1997.

Bergsten, C. Fred. "The Impact of the Euro on Exchange Rates and International Policy Cooperation," In *EMU and the International Monetary System*. Washington, D.C.: 1997.

Bertaut, Carol C., and M. F. Iyigun, "The Launch of the Euro." *Federal Reserve Bulletin*, Vol. 85, No. 10, Oct. 1999.

Bordo, Michael D., and L. Jonung. "The Future of EMU: What Does the History of Monetary Unions Tell Us?" NBER Working Paper No. W7365, Sep. 1999.

Buiter, Willem. "Six Months in the Life of the Euro: What Have We Learnt?" Speech. June 29, 1999.

Buiter, Willem, G. Corsetti, and P. Pesenti. *Financial Markets and European Monetary Cooperation: The Lessons of the 1992-1993 Exchange Rate Mechanism Crisis*. Cambridge, England: Cambridge University Press, 1998.

Corsetti, Giancarlo, and P. Pesenti. "Stability, Asymmetry and Discontinuity: The Outset of European Monetary Union." Brookings Paper on Economic Activity. Washington, D.C.: Sep. 1999.

De Bandt, Oliver, and E.P. Davis. "A Cross-Country Comparison of Market Structures In European Banking," Working Paper No. 7, Frankfurt: European Central Bank, Sep. 1999.

de la Dehesa, Guillermo, and P.B. Kenen. *EMU Prospects*. Washington, D.C.: Group of Thirty, Occasional Paper 50, 1995.

Duisenberg, Willem F. "The Eurosystem's Strategy for the Euro," Speech. Mar. 12, 1999.

Duisenberg, Willem F., "The Euro, the Dollar and National Economic Policies: What Room for Manoeuvre?" Speech. Mar. 25, 1999.

Duisenberg, Willem F. "Developments in the Financial Sector Following the Introduction of the Euro." Speech. June 3, 1999.

Duisenberg, Willem F., "The Single European Monetary Policy," Speech. Sep. 2, 1999.

Duisenberg, Willem F., "The ESCB and the Federal Reserve System: Comparing Structures and Methods," Speech. Apr. 29, 1997.

Eichengreen, Barry. "Europe's Role In International Financial Markets After EMU." Conference speech. Oct. 1997.

Eudey, Gwen. "Why Is Europe Forming A Monetary Union?" *Business Review* Federal Reserve Bank of Philadelphia Nov./Dec. 1998.

Feldstein, Martin. "EMU and International Conflict." *Foreign Affairs*, Vol. 76, No. 6, Nov./Dec. 1997.

Folkerts-Landau, D.; D. Mathieson, D.; and G. Schinasi. "European Monetary Union: Institutional Framework for Financial Policies and Structural Implications." *International Capital Markets: Developments, Prospects, and Key Policy Issues.* Washington, D.C.: IMF, Nov. 1997.

Frieden, Jeffry. "The Euro: Who Wins? Who Loses?" *Foreign Policy* Fall 1998.

Friedrich, Klaus. "Consequences of EMU for Europe." Testimony before the Committee on Banking and Financial Services. Washington, D.C.: April 24, 1998.

Goodhart, Charles A.E. "The Transition to EMU," *Scottish Journal of Political Economy* Vol. 43, No., 3 Aug. 1996.

Henning, C. Randall. *Cooperating with Europe's Monetary Union.* Washington, D.C.: Institute for International Economics, May 1997.

Henning, C. Randall, and P.C. Padoan. *Transatlantic Perspectives on the Euro.* Pittsburgh, Pennsylvania: European Community Studies Association, 2000.

Henning, C. Randall. "Europe's Monetary Union and the United States." *Foreign Policy* Spring 1996.

Issing, Otmar. "The Future Role of the Euro In the International Financial System." Speech. Oct. 24, 1997.

Karczmar, Mieczyslaw. "How Americans View the Euro." *The International Economy* Vol. 12, No. 5, Sep./Oct. 1998.

Kenen, Peter B. "Sorting Out Some EMU Issues." Reprints in International Finance No. 29. Princeton University, Dec. 1996.

Klein, Michael W. "European Monetary Union." *New England Economic Review* Mar./Apr. 1998.

Lannoo, Karel. "Financial Supervision in EMU." Bonn, Germany: Center for European Integration Studies, 1999.

Liebscher, Klaus. "European Economic and Monetary Union—Chances and Challenges for Europe." Speech. Apr. 1999.

Masson, Paul R., T. H. Kruege, and B. G. Turtelboom, eds., *EMU and the International Monetary System*, International Monetary Fund, 1997.

McCauley, Robert N. "The Euro and the Dollar," Basel, Switzerland: BIS Working Paper No. 50, Nov. 1997.

McCauley, Robert N. and W. R. White. "The Euro and European Financial Markets." In *EMU and the International Monetary System*. Washington, D.C.: IMF, 1997.

McDonough, William J. "A U.S. Perspective on Economic and Monetary Union in Europe," Speech. Frankfurt, Germany, Nov. 17, 1997.

Kaufman, George. *The U.S. Financial System: Money, Markets, and Institutions*. Prentice Hall: Englewood Cliffs, New Jersey, 1995.

Maikinen, Gail E. "Euro Currency: How Much Could It Cost the United States?" Washington, D.C.: Congressional Research Service, Dec. 21, 1998.

Maystadt, Philippe. "Implications of EMU for the IMF," In *EMU and the International Monetary System*. Washington, D.C.: 1997.

Meyer, Laurence H. "Challenges to the European Millennium." Speech. Apr. 26, 1999.

Mundell, Robert A. "The Euro: How Important?" *Cato Journal*, Vol. 18, No. 3, Winter 1999.

Padoa-Schioppa, Tommaso. "EMU and Banking Supervision." Lecture. Feb. 24, 1999.

Peterson, Michael. "What the Euro Means to America." Euromoney, June 1999.

Prati, Alessandro, and G.J. Schinasi. "EMU and International Capital Markets: Structural Implications and Risks," In *EMU and the International Monetary System*. Washington, D.C.: 1997.

Prati, Alessandro, and G. Schinasi. "Ensuring Financial Stability inn the Euro Area." *Finance & Development*, Dec. 1998.

Schieber, Helmut. "The International Role of the Euro." Speech. Sep. 21, 1998.

Solomon, Robert. "International Effects of the Euro." Policy Brief No. 42. Brookings Institution, Jan. 1999.

Stevens, Ed. "The Euro," *Economic Commentary* Federal Reserve Bank of Cleveland. Jan. 1, 1999.

Summers, Lawrence H., Testimony before Senate Budget Committee, Oct. 21, 1997.

Summers, Lawrence H., "EMU: An American View of Europe," Speech. Apr. 30, 1997.

Thiessen, Gordon. "The Euro: Its Economic Implications and Its Lessons for Canada." Speech. Jan. 20, 1999.

Tietmeyer, Hans. "The Euro: A Challenge To, And Opportunity For, the Financial Markets." Oct. 15, 1998.

Tietmeyer, Hans. "Whether the Euro Can Assume the Role of A Major International Currency." Speech. Oct. 28, 1997.

Truman, Edwin M. "The Single Currency and Europe's Role in the World Economy," Speech. Apr. 6, 1999.

Volcker, Paul A. "An American Perspective on EMU," In *EMU and the International Monetary System*. Washington, D.C.: 1997.

White, William R. "The Coming Transformation of Continental European Banking?" Working Paper No. 54. Basel, Switzerland: BIS, June 1998.

Wilson, Arlene. "European Monetary Union and the United States: An Overview." Washington, D.C.: Congressional Research Service, Mar. 24, 1999.

Wilson, Arlene. "European Monetary Union and the Euro: How Will the United States Be Affected?" Washington, D.C.: Congressional Research Service, Apr. 11, 1997.

Wilson, Arlene. "European Monetary Union; Economic Implications for the United States." Washington, D.C.: May 6, 1992.

Wynne, Mark A. "The European System of Central Banks," *Economic Review* Federal Reserve Bank of Dallas. First Quarter 1999.

## Other Documents

"Banking in the Euro Area: Structural Features and Trends," *ECB Monthly Bulletin* Apr. 1999.

"Could the Euro Put the ECB Under Pressure?" *ECB Observer* European Monetary Policy No. 72, Nov. 11, 1999.

Council of Economic Advisors. *Economic Report of the President*, Washington, D.C.:1999.

*Economic and Monetary Union: Compilation of Community Legislation.* Luxembourg: European Commission, 1999.

*EMU—Facts, Challenges and Policies*. Paris: Organization for Economic Cooperation and Development, 1999.

"EMU, the ECB and Financial Supervision." Statement No. 2. No Location: European Shadow Financial Regulatory Committee, Oct. 19, 1998.

"Monetary and Exchange Rate Policy Cooperation Between the Euro Area and Other EU Countries," Frankfurt: European Monetary Institute. Dec. 13, 1996.

"Possible Effects of EMU on the EU Banking Systems in the Medium and Long Term," Frankfurt: European Central Bank, Feb. 1999.

*Practical Issues Arising from the Euro.* London: Bank of England, Dec. 1999.

"The Euro Area One Year After the Introduction of the Euro: Key Characteristics and Changes in the Financial Structure," *ECB Monthly Bulletin* Jan. 2000.

"The Institutional Framework of the European System of Central Banks," *ECB Monthly Bulletin* Jul. 1999.

Wrightson Associates. "The Euro and the Dollar" *The Money Market Observer*, Jan. 8, 1999.

*69th Annual Report: 1 April 1998—31 March 1999.* Basle, Switzerland: Bank for International Settlements, June 7, 1999.

## Web sites

Bank for International Settlements: www.bis.org
European Central Bank: www.ecb.int
European Union: www.eu.int
U.S. Department of the Treasury: www.treas.gov
U.S. Department of State: www.state.gov
International Monetary Fund: www.imf.org

*Chapter 5*

# THE IMPACT OF THE CHANGEOVER TO THE EURO ON COMMUNITY POLICIES, INSTITUTIONS AND LEGISLATION

*European Commission: Economic and Financial Affairs*

## 1. BACKGROUND

On 5 November 1997, the Commission adopted a Communication entitled *The impact of the changeover to the euro on community policies, institutions and legislation.*[1] It provided an assessment of the practical consequences for Community policies as a result of the euro, the euro-compatibility of Community legislation, and the technical and operational consequences for the Commission (information technology, administrative changes, information and training of staff).

The Communication was limited to the implications of the euro on existing Community policies and legislation: it did not cover Community measures directly required for the introduction of the euro (e.g. legislation to establish the European Central Bank, the information program on the euro), nor ongoing/new policy initiatives in other fields which may be affected by the euro.

---

[1] COM(97)560 of 05.11.97

This note describes the progress made in implementing the Communication as on the date of the introduction of the euro on 1 January 1999. In the vast majority of cases, the strategy and deadlines described in the Communication are being adhered to.

On 6 October 1998, the European Parliament adopted its report (Langen) on the Communication, in which they request the Commission to provide the Parliament with a progress report. This report is in response to that request.

Part of the preparations described in the Communication have direct or indirect implications for other Community institutions and at Member State level, e.g. the transposition of Community Directives. To the extent possible, this note also summarizes their progress, but it is not comprehensive. However, the Directorate General for Economic and Financial Affairs has published an overview on the preparation of national public administration for the euro.[2]

# 2. IMPACTS OF THE CHANGEOVER IN CERTAIN SECTORAL AREAS

## 2.1 Community Budget

On 3 April 1998, the Commission proposed an amendment to the Financial Regulation[3] which provided for the Community budget to be drawn up and executed in euro as of 1 January 1999.[4] The Court of Auditors and the European Parliament gave their respective opinions in October 1998. The Commission adopted a revised proposal[5]. The final adoption by the Council took place on December 17, 1998 and the regulation entered into force on January 1, 1999[6].

---

[2] Euro Paper N° 27, July 1998: Fact sheets on the preparation of national administrations to the euro (status – 15 May 1998)

[3] COM(98)324

[4] Apart from changes required for the introduction of the euro, there were two other elements in this proposal: arrangements for any pecuniary sanctions arising under the Stability and Growth Pact and separate budgetary arrangements for the Committee of Regions and the Economic and Social Committee. This last element was postponed by the Council until mid-1999.

[5] COM(98)676

[6] O.J. L 347, 23.12.1998

## 2.2 Agricultural Policy

A new agrimonetary regime and measures allowing for the transition of the old system to the new one were proposed by the Commission on June 10 1998[7]. The Council decided along the lines of the proposals on 15 December 1998 by Regulations EC/2799/98 establishing agrimonetary arrangements for the euro[8] and EC/2800/98 on transitional measures to be applied under the common agricultural policy with a view to the introduction of the euro[9]. The new system abandons green rates in favor of using the fixed conversion rates for participating currencies and market exchange rates for the "pre-ins". In order to ensure a smooth transition to the introduction of the euro, a scheme of temporary agrimonetary compensation for reductions in prices and direct payments is introduced. This process will be completed by the end of 2001. The agrimonetary regime for the Member States not part of the euro area maintains the principles concerning compensations for income losses caused by appreciations of the "pre-in" currencies vis-à-vis the euro. However, these compensations are limited to appreciations occurring before 31 December 2001; the third and the last tranche of compensation could be granted in 2004 at the latest.

The detailed rules for the application of the agrimonetary system for the euro in agriculture are covered by the Commission Regulation EC2808/98.[10] Commission regulation EC/2813/98[11] covers the detailed rules for applying the transitional measures for the introduction of the euro into the common agricultural policy.

## 2.3 Administrative Expenditure

Four Council Regulations[12] have been adopted amending the Staff Regulations and the conditions of employment of other officials provide for all salaries, pensions and other remunerations to be established in euro as from 1 January 1999.

These Regulations anticipated to this date the conversion into euros of the parameters for calculating the remuneration and pensions (basic salary,

---

[7] JO C 224 of 17.7.1998, p. 15
[8] JO L 349 of 24.12.1998, p.1
[9] JO L 349 of 24.12.1998, p.8
[10] JO L 349 of 24.12.1998, p.36
[11] JO L 349 of 24.12.1998, p.48
[12] SN/3617/98, SN/3618/982458, 2459, 2460, and 2461 of 12 November 1998 (OJ L307 of 17.11.98)

allowances, contributions, tax, exchange rates applied to salaries, etc.) and other entitlements. These amounts were converted on 1.01.99 and published as a Commission Communication[13] in the Official Journal of the European Communities[14].

The same regulations provided that, while payments in non-participating countries will continue to be made in the national currency, payments to officials and pensioners based in participating countries are made in euro.

Salaries applying to members of the institutions (Commissioners, Members of the Court of Justice, of the Court of First Instance and of the Court of Auditors etc..) were converted at the same time. The members' indemnities are fixed by a separate regulation, which required a similar change[15] of Belgian Franc references to the euro. The Community Rules on the sickness insurance and accident insurance schemes (RCAM) for Community officials have been modified for the euro to become the unit of account as of January 1999. This required two Decisions[16] by general agreement of all Community institutions, which was recorded by the Court of Justice on 17.12.98.

## 3. COMMUNITY LEGISLATION AND POLICIES

### 3.1 The Legal Framework for the Euro

Three Regulations have been adopted. Council Regulation 1103/97 on certain provisions relating to the introduction of the euro[17] was adopted in June 1997, and immediately entered into force. It contains provisions dealing with ECU-euro conversions, the continuity of contracts as well as rounding and conversion rules. Council Regulation 974/98 on the introduction of the euro[18] was adopted in May 1998. It entered into force on 1 January 1999, and contains provisions on the use of the euro during the transitional period (no compulsion / no prohibition), banknotes and coins and the final changeover to the euro on 1 January 2002.

The fixed conversion rates were adopted by the Council on 31 December 1998, and entered into force on 1 January 1999.[19]

---

[13] 1999/C 60/09
[14] OJ C 60/11 of 2.3.1999
[15] Reg. 2778/98 of 17.12.98 (OJ 347 of 23.12.98)
[16] docs 10551/98 STAT 33 FIN 256 and 10552/98 STAT 34 FIN 257
[17] OJ L 162 of 19.06.1997
[18] OJ L 139 of 11.05.98
[19] Council regulation EC/2866/98. OJ L 359 of 31.12.98

## 3.2 Internal Market

***Internal market legislation:*** most of the euro impact on internal market legislation has already been dealt with through agreed interpretative clarification. The remaining small number of cases will be dealt with through legislative changes, either using revision mechanisms already existing in the legislation or, if necessary, through new amending proposals.

***Export credits:*** DG I has reached unanimous agreement with Member States and other participants in the arrangement on guidelines for officially supported Export Credits (OECD) on a new system of minimum interest rates (CIRRs) to be applied under the OECD Consensus. Member States have agreed that a single euro CIRR should prevail for all participating countries (instead of a series of national CIRRs). The Commission's proposal to base the minimum rates on the funding cost of first-class sovereign borrowers belonging to the euro zone has also been accepted. In practice, this means that the base rate of the euro CIRR will correspond to the secondary market yield of government bonds issued by participating Member States with the highest credit standing. Eurostat calculates on a daily basis a euro yield curve and precise yields for different credit terms. The basis for the curve is bonds with a total market value of 800.000 million euro. DG I takes care of external notifications.

***The euro-vignette*** is a common system, based on a Community Directive,[20] for charging goods vehicles for using the motorway network; it covers six Member States (B, D, DK, L, NL, S). The Directive provides for amounts in ECU to be converted into national currencies using the exchange rate applying on 1 October of the preceding year. The question arose whether the cost in national currency units of 1999 vignettes in the four euro-area countries (B, D, L, NL) should be calculated on the basis of the existing system (i.e. their exchange rates vis à vis the ECU on 1 October 1998) or using the fixed conversion rates which will apply from 1 January 1999. The Commission proposed to apply the existing system for the year 1999, with "in" Member States using the fixed conversion rates for euro-vignettes in 2000. No changes would occur for nonparticipating countries. Member States endorsed the Commission proposal on 5 November 1998.

***VAT, customs and the single administrative document:*** to date no specific legislative action has been tabled in the field of VAT or excise duties related to the introduction of the euro. The Commission will reflect on the need for legislative action during the transitional period with a view to

---

[20] Directive 93/89/EEC

tackling any discrepancies arising from the application of currency conversion clauses. Regarding the Single Administrative Document (SAD), the Commission has amended Regulation 2454/93 (fixing the implementation rules for Regulation 2913) giving the Member States the right to introduce the changes required.[21]

***Consumer protection:*** The Directives on consumer credit and certain other contracts[22] contain conversion clauses for threshold amounts in ECU into national currencies. For countries participating in the euro zone, these amounts shall be brought into line at the revision dates provided for in the Directives. Directive 87/102 provides for a revision to take place every five years, and thus will occur in 2000 during the transitional period.

***External relations:*** given the principle of lex monatae, it is not necessary to alter international agreements which contain references to the euro or participating national currencies. EC delegations in third countries have been provided with information on the euro: this will continue in 1999. DG II in the €uro Papers series has published several documents of particular relevance to third countries.[23]

## 4. OPERATIONAL ASPECTS OF THE CHANGEOVER

### 4.1 Treasury and Financial Management

DG XIX is continuing its policy to express all contracts, and corresponding payment operations, in /euros to the extent possible, notably to avoid rounding errors which might arise from double conversions. This is notably the case when invoices expressed in national currency units are being paid out in euro units (and subsequently converted back if the creditor's account is expressed in NCUs).

Regarding Structural Fund payments, Commission Regulation 1866/90, as amended, requires Member States to inform the Commission of the account to which they wish their payments from the Structural Funds to be credited. Many Member States have asked for the payments to be made to commercial bank accounts, since the Treasury accounts with the Commission are denominated in national currencies whereas Structural

---

[21] Commission Regulation 1677/98 of 29.07.98, OJ L 212 of 30.07.98
[22] Directive 85/577/EEC, Directive 87/102/EEC as amended by Directive 98/7/EEC
[23] Euro paper N° 1 'External aspects of EMU': N° 15 'The legal implications of EMU under US and New York' law: N° 24 'The impact of the euro on Mediterranean countries': N° 26 'The implication of the introduction of the euro for non-EU countries.'

Funds payments are made in ECU. Letters were sent on 1 October 1998 to the Member States asking whether they wished to change their instructions when the euro is introduced. Some Member States changed their instructions.

Letters were also sent on 1 October 1998 to the Member States asking whether they intended to credit the own resources to the Commission's accounts held in the Treasuries in euro or in national currency units. Six Member States are using the euro. Discussions have been held with the ECB on the opening of an account for the Commission which could simplify its financial operations.

Tests were made with the banks to ensure that they would be able to process the payment files in euro which would be sent to them by the Commission as from January 1999. These tests were successfully completed and the payment of salaries in euros are being made without problems.

"Infor écu", a currency list published on a monthly basis by DG XIX, has been retitled "Infor euro". The order of currencies and the section headings have been adapted accordingly.

The Commission is giving prior notification to the ECB of foreign exchange operations above a certain level. The Commission is also sending a monthly report to the ECB of its operations completed.

## 4.2 Statistics

Eurostat has proposed that, as far as the conversion of historical series is concerned, the following rules should be observed:

- Series in national currencies

Series stored in the databases of Eurostat expressed in national currencies will continue in the same denomination, at least until 31 December 2001. They will not be converted into euro with the irrevocably fixed conversion rates.

- Series in ECU

As far as statistical series in ECU in Eurostat's databases are concerned, they will be left unchanged. Series established after 1 January 1999 will be denominated in euro. The euro series will be the statistical continuation of the ECU series. This will be highlighted by:

- a new title for denomination for all euro series/tables where the label is ECU up to 31 December 1998 and euro from 1 January 1999
- brief footnotes for users
- Series converted with the irrevocably fixed conversion rate

It is necessary to introduce a labelling convention for converted series with the irrevocably fixed conversion rate. This will avoid misunderstandings that might arise when Member States publish back data converted into euro, using the fixed conversion rate, while the same data is appearing in Eurostat and Commission series in ECU. Obviously, the statistical nature of the two series will not be the same: for example, converted series cannot be used for comparisons of levels or aggregations among countries. To solve this problem, Eurostat has proposed the following convention on the labelling of all series in national currency converted into euro at the constant euro exchange rate of 1 January 1999:

All data before 1 January 1999 expressed in the currency of one of the countries that has introduced the euro and converted into euro using the conversion rate will be labelled euroXXX (eg Germany: euroDEM). XXX refers to the ISO code of the national currencies of the different countries. The official list of acronyms is:

|  |  |
|---|---|
| Belgium | BEF |
| Denmark | DKK |
| Germany | DEM |
| Greece | GRD |
| Spain | ESP |
| France | FRF |
| Ireland | IEP |
| Italy | ITL |
| Luxembourg | LUF |
| The Netherlands | NLG |
| Austria | ATS |
| Portugal | PTE |
| Finland | FIM |
| Sweden | SEK |
| United Kingdom | GBP |

## 4.3. Informatics

The inter-service group "EURO/YEAR 2000", chaired by the Informatics Directorate, ensures the co-ordination of activities in both areas. Concerning the euro, the necessary adaptations to the Commission's information systems were terminated in time, especially for those being of importance by the beginning of 1999.

A working group with the other institutions has been created by the Informatics Directorate to exchange experiences and co-ordinate technical activities concerning the euro and the year 2000. The inter-institutional group has ensured the necessary coordination of technical plans for the changeover in January 1999.

In the area of administrative systems (payroll, mission and medical expenses) the euro has been successfully introduced as of January 1999.

As a result of the activities of DG III and the Informatics Directorate, the international standardization bodies have approved the euro symbol € and the Informatics Directorate has integrated it into the Commission's standard informatics configuration that was deployed at the end of 1998. At the same time, practical and technical guides on the use of the euro have been distributed to all officials.

Given the scope and magnitude of the challenge facing the public sector IT community in adapting European information systems to the euro, the Informatics Directorate and DG III (IDA) organized a symposium with the Member States in June 1998. This symposium confirmed the need for public sector information exchange on the euro and IT. In particular it highlighted the need to co-ordinate changeover plans between the Commission and national and local administrations when their information systems are interlinked. The Informatics Directorate will organize a second symposium in June 1999 to review progress and promote further co-operation on the IT systems necessary for the euro in the public sector.

The Informatics Directorate also organized a joint conference with the Portuguese government in July 1998 on adapting information systems to the euro and the year 2000. This conference proposed the exchange and co-ordination of contingency plans regarding IT systems and the year 2000 and confirmed the need to allocate, as a top priority, the resources required to complete the adaptations necessary for both the euro and the year 2000 in due time. Similar conferences will be organized with other Member States and with SMEs.

## 5. INFORMATION AND TRAINING FOR STAFF

A staff training program covering all Community institutions was initiated in February 1998. It began with a series of articles in the staff journal *Commission en Direct* and was launched by President Santer. A survey on the awareness of staff on the euro was undertaken, and a questions and answers service was established which is run by DG II.

A second phase of the staff information campaign was conducted during Autumn 1998. In view of the comprehensive nature of the campaigns organized at national and sectoral level, the internal campaign focused on issues of specific interest to Community officials (e.g. changeover of remunerations and pensions).

In December 1998, all staff and pensioners of all Community institutions received a brochure prepared by DGs II, IX and X entitled *Our salaries, pensions and other allowances in euro*. This explained how salaries, pensions, mission expenses and medical expenses would convert to the euro. A series of interviews covering the Commission's internal changeover work in different areas (DGs VI, IX, XV, XIX, Eurostat,...) were published in *Commission en Direct*. Lunch time conferences were organized in Brussels and Luxembourg. In January 1999, Commission officials received a practical guide on the use of the euro. Some Directorates-General organized complementary staff information actions.

*Chapter 6*

# MEETING IN THE COMPOSITION OF HEADS OF STATE OR GOVERNMENT

## *Council of the European Union*

### DECISION ON THE PARTICIPATING COUNTRIES IN THE SINGLE CURRENCY

On the basis of the Council recommendation adopted the previous day and following the European Parliament's Opinion delivered in the morning, the Council -meeting in the composition of Heads of State or Government - unanimously decided that eleven Member States, namely, Belgium, Germany, Spain, France, Ireland, Italy, Luxembourg, The Netherlands, Austria, Portugal and Finland fulfil the necessary conditions for the adoption of the single currency on 1 January 1999. These countries will therefore participate in the third stage of Economic and Monetary Union.

Hailed as an historic step by all the Heads of State or Government, this decision marks the accomplishment of Economic and Monetary Union according to the timetable set out in the Treaty on European Union concluded at Maastricht in 1992.

Based on the European Monetary Institute and Commission reports, the Council confirmed the positive findings of the Ecofin Council for the eleven countries which can be summarized as follows :

- national legislation, including the statute of the national central bank, is compatible with the Treaty and the Statute of the European System of Central Banks (ESCB), or, all the necessary steps have been taken to ensure that this is the case at the time of establishment of the ESCB, as the Treaty requires;
- the average rate of inflation in the year ending January 1998 was below the reference value;
- these countries are not subject to a Council Decision on the existence of an excessive government deficit;
- these countries have been members of the ERM for the last two years and their currencies have not been subject to severe tensions; the Italian lira and the Finnish markka joined the ERM only in October and November 1996 respectively; since entry these currencies have not been subject to severe tensions;
- in the year ending in January 1998, the long term interest rates in these countries were below the reference value.

The Council also stated that Greece and Sweden do not at this stage fulfil the necessary conditions.

The Council did not assess whether the United Kingdom and Denmark fulfil the conditions given that, in accordance with the relevant Treaty provisions the United Kingdom notified the Council that it does not intend to move to the third stage of EMU on 1 January 1999, and Denmark notified the Council that it will not participate in the third stage of the EMU.

On the individual Member States the Decision states the following :

## Belgium

In Belgium, national legislation, including the statute of the national central bank, is compatible with Articles 107 and 108 of the Treaty and the Statute of the European System of Central Banks (ESCB).

Regarding the fulfillment of the convergence criteria mentioned in the four indents of Article 109j(1) of the Treaty:

- the average inflation rate in Belgium in the year ending in January 1998 stood at 1,4%, which is below the reference value,
- Belgium is not the subject of a Council Decision on the existence of an excessive government deficit,

- Belgium has been a member of the Exchange Rate Mechanism (ERM) for the last two years; in that period, the Belgian franc (BEF) has not been subject to severe tensions and Belgium has not devalued, on its own initiative, the BEF bilateral central rate against any other Member State's currency,
- in the year ending in January 1998, the long-term interest rate in Belgium was, on average, 5,7%, which is below the reference value.

Belgium has achieved a high degree of sustainable convergence by reference to all four criteria.

Consequently, Belgium fulfils the necessary conditions for the adoption of the single currency.

## Germany

In Germany, national legislation, including the statute of the national central bank, is compatible with Articles 107 and 108 of the Treaty and the Statute of the ESCB.

Regarding the fulfillment of the convergence criteria mentioned in the four indents of Article 109j(1) of the Treaty:

- the average inflation rate in Germany in the year ending in January 1998 stood at 1,4%, which is below the reference value,
- Germany is not the subject of a Council Decision on the existence of an excessive government deficit,
- Germany has been a member of the ERM for the last two years; in that period, the German mark (DEM) has not been subject to severe tensions and Germany has not devalued, on its own initiative, the DEM bilateral central rate against any other Member State's currency,
- in the year ending in January 1998, the long-term interest rate in Germany was, on average, 5,6%, which is below the reference value.

Germany has achieved a high degree of sustainable convergence by reference to all four criteria.

Consequently, Germany fulfils the necessary conditions for the adoption of the single currency.

## Greece

In Greece, national legislation, including the statute of the national central bank, is compatible with Articles 107 and 108 of the Treaty and the Statute of the ESCB.

Regarding the fulfillment of the convergence criteria mentioned in the four indents of Article 109j(1) of the Treaty:

- the average inflation rate in Greece in the year ending in January 1998 stood at 5,2%, which is above the reference value,
- the Council decided on 26 September 1994 that an excessive government deficit exists in Greece and this Decision has not been abrogated,
- the currency of Greece did not participate in the ERM in the two years ending in February 1998; during this period, the Greek drachma (GRD) has been relatively stable against the ERM currencies but it has experienced, at times, tensions which have been counteracted by temporary increases in domestic interest rates and by foreign exchange intervention. The GRD joined the ERM in March 1998,
- in the year ending in January 1998, the long-term interest rate in Greece was, on average, 9,8%, which is above the reference value.

Greece does not fulfil any of the convergence criteria mentioned in the four indents of Article 109j(1).

Consequently, Greece does not fulfil the necessary conditions for the adoption of the single currency.

## Spain

In Spain, national legislation, including the statute of the national central bank, is compatible with Articles 107 and 108 of the Treaty and the Statute of the ESCB.

Regarding the fulfillment of the convergence criteria mentioned in the four indents of Article 109j(1) of the Treaty:

- the average inflation rate in Spain in the year ending in January 1998 stood at 1,8%, which is below the reference value,

- Spain is not the subject of a Council Decision on the existence of an excessive government deficit,
- Spain has been a member of the ERM for the last two years; in that period, the Spanish peseta (ESP) has not been subject to severe tensions and Spain has not devalued, on its own initiative, the ESP bilateral central rate against any other Member State's currency,
- in the year ending in January 1998 the long-term interest rate in Spain was, on average, 6,3%, which is below the reference value.

Spain has achieved a high degree of sustainable convergence by reference to all four criteria.

Consequently, Spain fulfils the necessary conditions for the adoption of the single currency.

## France

France has taken all the necessary steps to make its national legislation, including the statute of the national central bank, compatible with Articles 107 and 108 of the Treaty and the Statute of the ESCB.

Regarding the fulfillment of the convergence criteria mentioned in the four indents of Article 109j(1) of the Treaty:

- the average inflation rate in France in the year ending in January 1998 stood at 1,2%, which is below the reference value,
- France is not the subject of a Council Decision on the existence of an excessive government deficit,
- France has been a member of the ERM for the last two years; in that period, the French franc (FRF) has not been subject to severe tensions and France has not devalued, on its own initiative, the FRF bilateral central rate against any other Member State's currency,
- in the year ending in January 1998, the long-term interest rate in France was, on average, 5,5%, which is below the reference value.

France has achieved a high degree of sustainable convergence by reference to all four criteria.

Consequently, France fulfils the necessary conditions for the adoption of the single currency.

## Ireland

In Ireland, national legislation, including the statute of the national central bank, is compatible with Articles 107 and 108 of the Treaty and the Statute of the ESCB.

Regarding the fulfillment of the convergence criteria mentioned in the four indents of Article 109j(1) of the Treaty:
- the average inflation rate in Ireland in the year ending in January 1998 stood at 1,2%, which is below the reference value,
- during the second stage of EMU, Ireland was not the subject of a Council Decision on the existence of an excessive government deficit,
- Ireland has been a member of the ERM for the last two years; in that period, the Irish pound (IEP) has not been subject to severe tensions and the IEP bilateral central rate has not been devalued against any other Member State's currency; on 16 March 1998, at a request of the Irish authorities, the bilateral central rates of the IEP against all other ERM currencies were revalued by 3%,
- in the year ending in January 1998, the long-term interest rate in Ireland was, on average, 6,2%, which is below the reference value.

Ireland has achieved a high degree of sustainable convergence by reference to all four criteria.

Consequently, Ireland fulfils the necessary conditions for the adoption of the single currency.

## Italy

In Italy, national legislation, including the statute of the national central bank, is compatible with Articles 107 and 108 of the Treaty and the Statute of the ESCB.

Regarding the fulfillment of the convergence criteria mentioned in the four indents of Article 109j(1) of the Treaty:

- the average inflation rate in Italy in the year ending in January 1998 stood at 1,8%, which is below the reference value,
- Italy is not the subject of a Council Decision on the existence of an excessive government deficit,

- Italy rejoined the ERM in November 1996; in the period from March 1996 to November 1996, the Italian lira (ITL) appreciated vis-à-vis the ERM currencies; since it re-entered the ERM, the ITL has not been subject to severe tensions and Italy has not devalued, on its own initiative, the ITL bilateral central rate against any other Member State's currency,
- in the year ending in January 1998, the long-term interest rate in Italy was, on average, 6,7%, which is below the reference value.

Italy fulfils the convergence criteria mentioned in the first, second and fourth indents of Article 109j(1); as regards the criterion mentioned in the third indent of Article 109j(1), the ITL, although having rejoined the ERM only in November 1996, has displayed sufficient stability in the last two years. For these reasons, Italy has achieved a high degree of sustainable convergence.

Consequently, Italy fulfils the necessary conditions for the adoption of the single currency.

## Luxembourg

Luxembourg has taken all the necessary steps to make its national legislation, including the statute of the national central bank, compatible with Articles 107 and 108 of the Treaty and the Statute of the ESCB.

Regarding the fulfillment of the convergence criteria mentioned in the four indents of Article 109j(1) of the Treaty:

- the average inflation rate in Luxembourg in the year ending in January 1998 stood at 1,4%, which is below the reference value,
- during the second stage of EMU, Luxembourg was not the subject of a Council Decision on the existence of an excessive government deficit,
- Luxembourg has been a member of the ERM for the last two years; in that period, the Luxembourg franc (LUF) has not been subject to severe tensions and Luxembourg has not devalued, on its own initiative, the LUF bilateral central rate against any other Member State's currency,
- in the year ending in January 1998, the long-term interest rate in Luxembourg was, on average, 5,6%, which is below the reference value.

Luxembourg has achieved a high degree of sustainable convergence by reference to all four criteria.

Consequently, Luxembourg fulfils the necessary conditions for the adoption of the single currency.

## The Netherlands

In the Netherlands, national legislation, including the statute of the national central bank, is compatible with Articles 107 and 108 of the Treaty and the Statute of the ESCB.

Regarding the fulfillment of the convergence criteria mentioned in the four indents of Article 109j(1) of the Treaty:

- the average inflation rate in the Netherlands in the year ending in January 1998 stood at 1,8%, which is below the reference value,
- the Netherlands is not the subject of a Council Decision on the existence of an excessive government deficit,
- the Netherlands has been a member of the ERM for the last two years; in that period, the Netherlands guilder (NLG) has not been subject to severe tensions and the Netherlands has not devalued, on its own initiative, the NLG bilateral central rate against any other Member State's currency,
- in the year ending in January 1998, the long-term interest rate in the Netherlands was, on average, 5,5%, which is below the reference value.

The Netherlands has achieved a high degree of sustainable convergence by reference to all four criteria.

Consequently, the Netherlands fulfils the necessary conditions for the adoption of the single currency.

## Austria

In Austria, national legislation, including the statute of the national central bank, is compatible with Articles 107 and 108 of the Treaty and the Statute of the ESCB.

Regarding the fulfillment of the convergence criteria mentioned in the four indents of Article 109j(1) of the Treaty:

- the average inflation rate in Austria in the year ending in January 1998 stood at 1,1%, which is below the reference value,
- Austria is not the subject of a Council Decision on the existence of an excessive government deficit,
- Austria has been a member of the ERM for the last two years; in that period, the Austrian schilling (ATS) has not been subject to severe tensions and Austria has not devalued, on its own initiative, the ATS bilateral central rate against any other Member State's currency,
- in the year ending in January 1998, the long-term interest rate in Austria was, on average, 5,6%, which is below the reference value.

Austria has achieved a high degree of sustainable convergence by reference to all four criteria.

Consequently, Austria fulfils the necessary conditions for the adoption of the single currency.

## Portugal

In Portugal, national legislation, including the statute of the national central bank, is compatible with Articles 107 and 108 of the Treaty and the Statute of the ESCB.

Regarding the fulfillment of the convergence criteria mentioned in the four indents of Article 109j(1) of the Treaty:

- the average inflation rate in Portugal in the year ending in January 1998 stood at 1,8%, which is below the reference value,
- Portugal is not the subject of a Council Decision on the existence of an excessive government deficit,
- Portugal has been a member of the ERM for the last two years; in that period, the Portuguese escudo (PTE) has not been subject to severe tensions and Portugal has not devalued, on its own initiative, the PTE bilateral central rate against any other Member State's currency,
- in the year ending in January 1998, the long-term interest rate in Portugal was, on average, 6,2%, which is below the reference value.

Portugal has achieved a high degree of sustainable convergence by reference to all four criteria.

Consequently, Portugal fulfils the necessary conditions for the adoption of the single currency.

## Finland

In Finland, national legislation, including the statute of the national central bank, is compatible with Articles 107 and 108 of the Treaty and the Statute of the ESCB.

Regarding the fulfillment of the convergence criteria mentioned in the four indents of Article 109j(1) of the Treaty:

- the average inflation rate in Finland in the year ending in January 1998 stood at 1,3%, which is below the reference value,
- Finland is not the subject of a Council Decision on the existence of an excessive government deficit,
- Finland has been a member of the ERM since October 1996; in the period from March 1996 to October 1996, the Finnish markka (FIM) appreciated vis-à-vis the ERM currencies; since it entered the ERM, the FIM has not been subject to severe tensions and Finland has not devalued, on its own initiative, the FIM bilateral central rate against any other Member State's currency,
- in the year ending in January 1998, the long-term interest rate in Finland was, on average, 5,9%, which is below the reference value.

Finland fulfils the convergence criteria mentioned in the first, second and fourth indents of Article 109j(1); as regards the convergence criterion mentioned in the third indent of Article 109j(1), the FIM, although having entered the ERM only in October 1996, has displayed sufficient stability in the last two years. For these reasons, Finland has achieved a high degree of sustainable convergence.

Consequently, Finland fulfils the necessary conditions for the adoption of the single currency.

## Sweden

In Sweden, national legislation, including the statute of the national central bank, is not compatible with Articles 107 and 108 of the Treaty and the Statute of the ESCB.

Regarding the fulfillment of the convergence criteria mentioned in the four indents of Article 109j(1) of the Treaty:

- the average inflation rate in Sweden in the year ending in January 1998 stood at 1,9%, which is below the reference value,
- Sweden is not the subject of a Council Decision on the existence of an excessive government deficit,
- the currency of Sweden has never participated in the ERM; in the two years under review, the Swedish krona (SEK) fluctuated against the ERM currencies reflecting among others the absence of an exchange rate target,
- in the year ending in January 1998, the long-term interest rate in Sweden was, on average, 6,5%, which is below the reference value.

Sweden fulfils the convergence criteria mentioned in the first, second and fourth indents of Article 109j(1) but does not fulfil the convergence criterion mentioned in the third indent thereof.

Consequently, Sweden does not fulfil the necessary conditions for the adoption of the single currency.

## APPOINTMENT OF THE MEMBERS OF THE EXECUTIVE BOARD OF THE EUROPEAN CENTRAL BANK

The Heads of State or Government reached a political understanding on the persons to be recommended as President, Vice-President and other members of the Executive Board of the European Central Bank. Therefore, the ensuing Ecofin Council will adopt the recommendation on these appointments (Mr Wim DUISENBERG as President for eight years, Mr Christian NOYER as Vice-President for four years, Mr Otmar ISSING as member for eight years, Mr Tommaso PADOA SCHIOPPA as member for seven years, Mr Eugenio DOMINGO SOLANS, as member for six years and Mrs Sirkka HÄMÄLÄINEN as member for five years).

## Oral statement by Mr Duisenberg, President of the European Monetary Institute

"I want to thank you for the honor of nominating me for the function of President of the ECB on this historic occasion.

I explained to the President of the European Council that I will, in view of my age, not want to serve the full term.

On the other hand it is my intention to stay at least to see through the transitional arrangements for the introduction of the euro notes and coins and the withdrawal of the national notes and coins, in accordance with the arrangements as agreed at Madrid.

I wish to emphasize that this is my decision and my decision alone and it is entirely of my own free will and mine alone and not under pressure from anyone that I have decided not to serve the full term. Also in the future the decision to resign will be my decision alone.

This must be clearly understood."

The President of the Council reported that there was agreement that the successor to Mr Duisenberg would be a French nomination for a period of eight years. In this context, Mr Jacques Chirac informed the Council that the French candidate would be Mr Jean-Claude Trichet.

Following consultation of the European Parliament and the European Monetary Institute, these nominations will be confirmed by consensus of Heads of State or Government of participating Member States before 1 July 1998 after which the European Central Bank is established.

## Statement of the Heads of State or Government on appointments to the Executive Board of the European Central Bank

While reaffirming the Treaty requirement to make appointments from persons of recognized standing and professional experience in monetary or banking matters, and the roles of the European Parliament and the Governing Council of the European Central Bank, the Heads of State or Government will give appropriate weight and appropriate consideration, according to a balanced principle of rotation, in their future decisions under Article 109a(2), to the recommendations for nationals of Member States which do not provide members of the Executive Board appointed in accordance with Article 50 of the ECB Statute.

# INDEX

## A

accession, 21, 49
accident insurance schemes, 90
adopted legislation, 76
agricultural policy, 89
agriculture, 42, 89
agrimonetary compensation, 89
agrimonetary regime, 89
agrimonetary system, 89
appreciation, 28
approved securities, 51
Automated Teller Machines (ATMs), 1, 15, 19, 21

## B

balance of payments, 28, 38
Bank for International Settlements (BIS), 43-45, 57-59, 64, 73, 83-85
bank loans, 59, 80
banking system, 31, 62, 64
banking systems, 62, 65
banknotes, 1, 2, 4, 7, 9-12, 14-16, 90
Belgium, 1, 17, 33, 94, 97-99
bilateral central rate, 77, 99, 101-106
Board of Governors, 26, 53, 74
broad-based assessment, 52
budget deficits, 20, 42

## C

Canada, 27, 34, 58, 65, 72, 84
capital flows, 49, 55, 57
capital markets, 57, 62
central banks, 9, 18, 20, 34, 42, 43, 47, 49-51, 54, 55, 64, 73, 77, 79, 80
coins, 1, 2, 4, 7, 9, 10, 12-15, 26, 36, 42, 90, 108
common market, 42
community budget, 88
community directives, 88
competition, 7, 9, 62, 63, 65, 69
contingency plans, 95
conversion rates, 16, 42, 89-91, 93
copyright protection, 4
Council of Economic Advisors, 84
Court of Auditors, 88, 90
Court of Justice, 90
cross-border euro payments, 46
currency markets, 49
currency reserves, 34, 47, 49, 50
currency value, 36, 54

## D

debt instruments, 61
depreciation, 55

developed countries, 50
developing countries, 46, 50
developing country currency reserves, 50
Directorate General for Economic and Financial Affairs, 88
distribution of cash, 15
domestic currency, 44, 47, 49, 78
drugs, 28, 29

## E

economic activity, 53
Economic and Monetary Union (EMU), 2, 17, 18, 20, 21, 38-42, 49, 51, 55-57, 59, 61-64, 69, 72, 73, 75, 77, 79, 81-85, 92, 97, 98, 102, 103
economic conditions, 20, 21, 34, 52-54
economic growth, 22, 34, 47, 51, 53, 56, 68, 69, 79
economic integration, vii, 19, 33, 34, 38, 71
economic policies, 34, 38, 41
economic prosperity, 2
economists, 21, 54
EU Treaty, 76
euro area, 2, 3, 7, 10, 12, 14, 15, 17, 35-51, 54-62, 64, 65, 67-71, 73, 76, 77, 79, 80, 89
euro payments, 46
European Bank for Reconstruction and Development (EBRD), 73
European Central Bank (ECB), 3, 4, 9, 10, 12, 14, 17, 18, 20, 22, 33, 36-38, 42, 46, 47, 49-52, 54, 55, 58, 63, 64, 69, 72-77, 81, 84, 85, 93, 87, 107, 108
European Community, 4, 18, 21, 38, 42, 77, 82
European Council, 3, 9, 37, 42, 75, 76, 108

European Currency Unit (ECU), 48, 76, 77, 90-94
European Economic Community (EEC), 42, 77, 91, 92
European Monetary Institute (EMI), 9, 18, 38, 42, 75, 77, 85, 97, 108
European Parliament, 37, 38, 76, 88, 97, 108
European System of Central Banks (ESCB), 3, 17, 18, 49, 51, 54, 77, 82, 84, 85, 98-107
European Union (EU), vii, 1-4, 7, 9, 17-21, 33-43, 46, 48, 49, 51, 54, 57, 61-65, 72-77, 79, 85, 97
Eurosystem, 3, 10, 17, 18, 81
Eurozone, 19, 20, 21, 22
Exchange Rate Mechanism (ERM), 37, 40, 77, 81, 98, 99-107
exchange rate(s), 2, 20, 21, 30, 34, 36, 37, 41, 46-49, 53-57, 61, 68, 69, 72, 74, 78, 89-91, 94, 107
exchange reserves, 79
expansion, 31

## F

Federal Reserve System, 26, 52, 53, 82
Federal Reserve, vii, 25-27, 29, 31, 32, 34, 47, 52, 53, 74, 81-84
financial institutions, 18, 51, 52, 63
financial markets, 33, 34, 39, 56, 57, 59, 62, 74
financial regulation, 88
financial services, 34, 40, 57-59, 63
fiscal polic(y)ies, 20, 30, 39, 61, 69
fluctuations, 39, 54, 55
foreign direct investment (FDI), 40, 55, 69-71, 78
foreign exchange markets, 46, 47, 54, 78
foreign exchange reserves, 48, 49, 77, 79

foreign exchange, 3, 28, 46, 47-49, 53, 54, 61-63, 77-79, 93, 100
foreign investment, 71
foreign investors, 33
foreign reserves, 49, 50
France, 1, 17, 20, 33, 34, 40, 65, 70, 72, 94, 97, 101

## G

Germany, 1, 3, 10, 17, 33, 34, 40, 65, 70, 72, 82, 83, 94, 97, 99
global economy, 42
global foreign currency reserves, 50
goods and services, vii, 22, 25-29, 31, 35
Governing Council of the ECB, 51, 76
government bonds, 61, 91
government debt, 20, 37, 60, 61
government deficit, 37, 98, 99-107
Greek drachma (GRD), 16, 94, 100
green rates, 89
gross domestic product (GDP), vii, 19, 20, 35-37, 39, 55

## H

Harmonized Index of Consumer Prices (HICP), 37

## I

imports, 28
income losses, 89
industrialized countries, 34, 43, 50
inflation rates, 37
inflation, 20-22, 30, 37, 40, 42, 47, 51-53, 98-107
informatics directorate, 95
information exchange, 43, 95
information technology, 87
insurance, 64, 70, 90
integration, 21, 33, 39, 46, 79

interest rate, 37, 40, 46, 51, 61, 99-107
interest rates, 20, 22, 28, 37, 51, 53, 55, 61, 91, 98, 100
international bond, 59
international financial institutions, 73
international financial system, 73
international markets, 51, 68
International Monetary Fund (IMF), 48, 50, 57, 58, 60, 63, 73, 74, 81, 82, 83, 85
International Organization for Standardization (ISO), 9, 17, 94
international trade, 43, 50, 68
introduction of the euro, 34, 39, 52, 57, 60, 61, 68, 72, 75, 87-92, 108
investments, 47, 64
Italy, 1, 17, 33, 34, 65, 72, 94, 97, 102, 103

## J

Japan, 34, 72
Journal of the European Communities, 90

## L

labor markets, 39
Latin America, 49
legacy currencies, 19
liberalization, 61
liquidity, 50, 57

## M

macroeconomic policies, 54, 56
macroeconomic policy, 72
Member States, 1-4, 7, 9, 15, 17, 18, 89, 91-95, 97, 98, 108
merchandise, 65
monetary issues, 77
monetary policies, 3, 47, 51

monetary policy, 2, 3, 17, 20, 22, 26, 28, 30, 33, 34, 36, 38, 40-42, 47, 51-55, 63, 74, 76, 77, 79

## N

national central banks (NCBs), 3, 10, 14, 15, 17, 18, 49, 51, 52
national currencies, vii, 4, 19, 20, 36, 39, 44, 45, 48-50, 54, 60-63, 91-94
national currency, 15, 16, 42, 90, 91, 92, 93, 94
national policies, 38
Netherlands guilder (NLG), 94, 104
new coins, 2, 10, 15, 21
new currency, 2, 19, 25, 31, 35, 62
North America, 57

## O

OECD Consensus. Member States, 91
official currency, 48
official reserves, 77
oil, 43, 53
open market, 51, 53
Organization for Economic Cooperation and Development (OECD), 73, 84, 91
overseas, 22

## P

participating currencies, 2, 89
payment systems, 3
pensioners, 90, 96
policymakers, 22, 34
political guidance, 76
price level, 27, 28, 30
price stability, 3, 17, 20, 37, 51, 52, 69, 76, 79
private sector, 43
public administration, 88
public sector, 18, 95

## R

rate of growth, 52
recession, 22, 32
recessions, 39
reference value, 52, 98-107
remunerations, 89, 96
Russia, 72

## S

savings, 61
securities markets, 53, 57
shopping, 15
short-term interest rates, 53
Single Administrative Document (SAD), 92
special drawing rights (SDR), 73
stock markets, 62
structural reform, 69
surveillance, 39
sustainable convergence, 99, 101-106

## T

taxes, 29, 38
terrorist attacks, 22
trade deficit, 28, 65
trade negotiations, 34, 72
trade relations, 49
Trans-European Automated Real-time Gross Settlement Express Transfer (TARGET), 46, 80

## U

U.S. dollar, 23, 34, 43, 45, 46
U.S. economy, 22, 23, 31, 32, 34, 47, 55
U.S. exports, 28, 68, 69
U.S. Federal Reserve, 22
U.S. firms, 69
U.S. imports, 28
U.S. trade, 33, 34, 65, 68, 69, 74

U.S. Treasury, 23, 28, 50, 60, 61
unemployment, 51, 52

wealth, 29, 30
working balances, 43
World Bank, 73